WORLD BANK WORKING PAPER NO. 127

Governance, Management, and Accountability in Secondary Education in Sub-Saharan Africa

Secondary Education in Africa (SEIA)

Africa Region Human Development Department

THE WORLD BANK
Washington, D.C.

Copyright © 2008
The International Bank for Reconstruction and Development / The World Bank
1818 H Street, N.W.
Washington, D.C. 20433, U.S.A.
All rights reserved
Manufactured in the United States of America
First Printing: January 2008

 printed on recycled paper

1 2 3 4 5 10 09 08 07

World Bank Working Papers are published to communicate the results of the Bank's work to the development community with the least possible delay. The manuscript of this paper therefore has not been prepared in accordance with the procedures appropriate to formally-edited texts. Some sources cited in this paper may be informal documents that are not readily available.

The findings, interpretations, and conclusions expressed herein are those of the author(s) and do not necessarily reflect the views of the International Bank for Reconstruction and Development/The World Bank and its affiliated organizations, or those of the Executive Directors of The World Bank or the governments they represent.

The World Bank does not guarantee the accuracy of the data included in this work. The boundaries, colors, denominations, and other information shown on any map in this work do not imply any judgment on the part of The World Bank of the legal status of any territory or the endorsement or acceptance of such boundaries.

The material in this publication is copyrighted. Copying and/or transmitting portions or all of this work without permission may be a violation of applicable law. The International Bank for Reconstruction and Development/The World Bank encourages dissemination of its work and will normally grant permission promptly to reproduce portions of the work.

For permission to photocopy or reprint any part of this work, please send a request with complete information to the Copyright Clearance Center, Inc., 222 Rosewood Drive, Danvers, MA 01923, USA, Tel: 978-750-8400, Fax: 978-750-4470, www.copyright.com.

All other queries on rights and licenses, including subsidiary rights, should be addressed to the Office of the Publisher, The World Bank, 1818 H Street NW, Washington, DC 20433, USA, Fax: 202-522-2422, email: pubrights@worldbank.org.

ISBN-13: 978-0-8213-7346-0
eISBN: 978-0-8213-7347-7
ISSN: 1726-5878   DOI: 10.1596/978-0-8213-7346-0

Cover photo by Jacob Bregman.

Library of Congress Cataloging-in-Publication Data has been requested

Contents

Foreword v
Acknowledgments vii
Acronyms and Abbreviations... ix
Executive Summary.. xi
Résumé analytique xvii

1. Introduction 1
2. International Trends Influencing Secondary Education in Sub-Saharan Africa 7
3. Issues of Governance in Secondary Education in Sub-Saharan Africa 13
4. Management of Secondary Education: Focus on the School 27
5. Accountability... 37
6. The Governance and Accountability of Private Schools 47
7. Special Issue: Addressing ICT and Technical Training 51
8. Recommendations 53

Appendixes
  A Terms of Reference.. 65
  B Years of Compulsory, Primary, Lower and Upper Secondary Education 67
  C Decentralization Matrix 69

Bibliography 71

List of Figures
1. Zambia Ministry of Education 20
2. Botswana Ministry of Education, Department of Secondary Education, Regional Structure.. 23

LIST OF BOXES

1. Decentralization 5
2. Decentralization to Schools 9
3. Defining Secondary Education 14
4. Vocational Training in Asia 14
5. Secondary Education: A Policy Challenge 16
6. Botswana: Successfully Planning for Expanded Secondary Education 18
7. Conclusions for Governance in the Education Ministry 26
8. School Improvement Plans in Senegal 34
9. South Africa's Experience with International Assessments 42
10. Procedure for Opening a Private School in Kenya 49

Foreword

Many African countries are undertaking important economic reforms, improving macroeconomic management, liberalizing markets and trade, and widening the space for private sector activity. Where such reforms have been sustained they produced economic growth and reduced poverty. However, Africa still faces serious development challenges in human development, notably in post-primary education. The World Bank incorporated this within its Africa Action Plan (AAP) by underscoring the fundamental importance of expanding not only primary but also secondary and higher education, and linking it to employment options for African youth.

The Education for All-Fast Track Initiative (EFA-FTI) involves over 30 bilateral and international agencies and has made important strides. In the coming years, the key challenges are to consolidate progress towards universal primary education and expand secondary school access in response to economic and social demands. Secondary education and training are prerequisites for increased economic growth and social development. It promotes productive citizenship and healthy living for young adolescents. To be competitive labor markets in Africa need more graduates with "modern knowledge and better skills." Asia and Latin America have shown these trends convincingly. However, expansion of post-primary education services while simultaneously improving its quality will require African countries to deliver these services more efficiently. Adoption of "innovative and best practices" from other Regions can help.

The "Secondary Education In Africa (SEIA)" study is part of the Africa Human Development Program that supports the Region's Africa Action Plan. Its objective is to assist countries to develop sustainable strategies for expansion and quality improvement in secondary education. The study program produced eight thematic studies, and additional papers, which were discussed at the regional SEIA conferences in which 38 countries and all major development partners participated (Uganda 2003; Senegal 2005; Ghana 2007). The SEIA Synthesis Report (2007) is a summary overview and discussion of all studies. All SEIA studies were produced with the help of national country teams and international institutions for which financial trust fund support is gratefully acknowledged. Study reports are available on the SEIA website: www.worldbank.org/afr/seia.

This thematic study is about governance, management and accountability in secondary education in Sub-Saharan Africa. It is based on country case studies from Senegal, South Africa, Uganda and Zambia as well as an extensive literature review. Increasingly the role of management and governance is recognized as important for providing and delivering effective services at all levels of education. At secondary education levels, in view of the growing demand for more and better services, these are crucial issues that need to be addressed urgently. Sub-Saharan Africa secondary education and training systems need to become more efficient and more effective. The current (unit) costs of junior and senior secondary education in most African countries prevent massive expansion of post-primary education. The objective is to present best practices for governance, management and accountability. I hope this report will make a timely and useful contribution.

Jacob Bregman
Lead Education Specialist and SEIA Task Team Leader
Africa Region Human Development (AFTHD)
The World Bank

Acknowledgments

The report was prepared by the American Institute for Research (AIR) and Khulisa Management, which oversaw the initial data collection for the three case studies. Field research for the three case studies was carried out by Dr. Ibrahima Thioub and Myriam Augustin in Senegal, Pat Sullivan in South Africa and Carol Coombe in Zambia. The main study report was drafted by Dr. Deborah Glassmann (AIR).

This thematic study report was prepared under the guidance of the SEIA Study Program team (Jacob Bregman, SEIA Team Leader and Lead Education Specialist, AFTHD). This SEIA thematic study was funded by the Norwegian and Irish Education Trust Funds, which are gratefully acknowledged.

The team is particularly grateful for the time and information provided by international colleagues whose knowledge and time made it possible to gather data unavailable in any published studies. At the World Bank, Jacob Bregman (SEIA Task Team Leader, AFTHD) and Adriaan Verspoor (Senior Consultant, Africa Region, World Bank) provided significant inputs and comments during several rounds of consultations. In addition to the SEIA team, a number of education staff in the World Bank provided time and very useful information.

Kathryn Toure, Regional Coordinator of the Education Research Network in West and Central Africa generously provided ERNWACA's technical report on the use of ICT in education in Benin, Cameroon, Ghana, Mali, and Senegal.

In Kenya, Juliana Nzomo formerly of the MOEST Planning Division, arranged for interviews in the MOEST in Nairobi with Mr. David Siele, Director, Secondary and Tertiary Education, Mary Njiroge, Director of Basic Education, John Njiroge of the Policy and Planning Division. Ali Atrash at the Kenya School Improvement Project in Mombasa provided extensive time for interviews, documents, and contacts with many colleagues and district officials, including Patrick Kanyoro, Community Development Office in the Kenya School Improvement Project, Juma Omwendo, Senior Education Officer, Municipal Education Office, and Khadija Said, the Principal of Sharif Nassir Girls' Secondary School in Mombasa. David Odongo, of the Community Rural Support Program provided useful insights into local school issues.

For the case study of Senegal, Sala Ba and Larraine Denakpo, at the Academy for Education Development provided several very useful contacts, including Mr. Falou Dieng, Head of Maurice Gueye Middle School near Dakar. Mr. Dieng provided numerous documents and hours of telephone conversation in response to questions.

For the case study of Zambia, Arnold Chengo and Terry Allsop deserve thanks for their time and insight into the secondary education system in that country.

A special thanks to Lorie Brush and Olivia Padilla of AIR for their support in the editing of this document.

Acronyms and Abbreviations

APU	Academic Production Unit
ADEA	Association for the Development of Education in Africa
BESSIP	Basic Education sub-Sector Investment Program
BOG	Board of Governors
BT	*Brevet de technicien,* first technical training degree
CAP	*Certificat d'aptitude professionnel,* second technical training degree
CEM	*Collège d'enseignement moyen,* Junior Secondary
CFA	West African community currency pegged to French franc
CRS	Comprehensive School Reform
DoE	Department of Education
DEB	District Education Board
DEO	District Education Officer
DRC	Democratic Republic of Congo
EMIS	Education Management Information System Program
ERNWACA	Education Research Network for West and Central Africa
ESA	Education Standards Agency
GER	Gross Enrollment Ratio
HSEB	High School Education Board
ICT	Information and Communication Technology
IFMIS	Integrated Financial Management Information System
JSSLE	Junior Secondary School Leaving Examination
KESSP	Kenya Education Sector Support Program
KIE	Kenya Institute of Education
KTSC	Kenya Teacher Service Commission
LAC	Latin America and the Caribbean
MOE	Ministry of Education
MOEST	Ministry of Education, Sports, and Training
OECD	Organisation for Economic Cooperation and Development
OLC	Open Learning Center
PDEF	*Programme Décennal d'éducation et de formation* (Ten-year Education and Training Program)
PEB	Provincial Education Board
PEO	Provincial Education Officer
PISA	Program for International Student Assessment
PRSP	Poverty Reduction Strategy Paper
PTA	Parent-Teacher Association
PETS	Public Expenditure Tracking System
SAGA	Semi-autonomous government agency
SDM	Shared Decision-Making
SDP	School Development Plan
SEIA	Secondary Education in Africa
SGB	School Governing Board or School Governing Body
SIP	School Improvement Plan
SMC	School Management Committee
SMT	School Management Team

TESSIP	Technical Education sub-Sector Investment Program
TIMSS	Trends in International Mathematics and Science Study
TSC	Teaching Service Commission
TVET	Technical and Vocational Education and Training
WSE	Whole School Evaluation

Executive Summary

Purpose of this Study

Education for All has led to a significant increase in the number of students completing primary education in Sub-Saharan Africa (SSA). It has also created tremendous demand for secondary education. This "highway" between primary and tertiary education faces many challenges worldwide. Largely designed in the developed world in the 19th and early 20th centuries, and transported to the developing world, secondary education is not well aligned with 21st century needs and purposes. Economies that are increasingly "knowledge-driven" need workers with extensive knowledge, developed skills, and increasingly the creativity and flexibility of an entrepreneur. Governments worldwide are experimenting with different ways of tracing and dividing the secondary highway into shorter or longer routes, with a more or less academic or vocational emphasis, with more or less involvement from the private sector. No single solution prevails for balancing the requirements of this knowledge economy with equally legitimate concerns for educational equity and a high quality of education services. As greater numbers of SSA primary school leavers seek to make the transition to secondary education, SSA governments must evaluate their secondary education governance, management, and accountability practices to ensure they can meet student and societal needs.

Definition of Terms

Governance, defined in different ways in the literature, in this report will address: (i) the structure and function of the secondary systems as a whole, (ii) the legislative and regulatory framework for education provision and governance, (iii) the structure, roles, and responsibilities of the central education ministry and its decentralized offices, and (iv) the local steering mechanisms for secondary schools (for example, boards of governors and parent-teacher associations). *Management* covers the processes and practices established by legislation or through practice to realize educational objectives at the level of the school and the community. *Accountability* refers to the processes by which the education system holds itself responsible for delivering the appropriate services and meeting its goals for educating students.

Trends Influencing Secondary Education in Sub-Saharan Africa

Internationally, many reforms in secondary education are being provoked by the incompatibility between a secondary education system developed in an industrial 19th century and the demands of a technological 21st century. The growing demand for education and the pressure for greater access, equity, and quality are also provoking education reforms. These pressures for change are affecting the governance, management, and accountability of secondary education. International trends and their effects on SSA can be summarized as follows.

Education of All (EFA). The EFA agenda has had a tremendous impact on secondary education: first by increasing the demand for secondary education and second by competing for precious resources necessary to expand and improve the quality of the secondary education system.

Demands of Globalization. The workplace in a globalizing world is demanding knowledge, skills and competencies such as problem-solving and the ability to analyze and apply information. It is also demanding expertise in information and communication technology (ICT). In consequence, ministries are reviewing and changing the objectives, structure, and curriculum of secondary education. Their struggle is to adapt an industrial model of secondary education to a modern world.

More Years of Education. More people are going to school longer worldwide, and the duration of basic, compulsory education is lengthening. The number of years of secondary education is also increasing to accommodate the explosion of new knowledge produced by rapidly developing technologies. Some SSA governments are extending free basic education, but no SSA governments provide universal free secondary education. The demand for more education has raised questions about the governance, management and accountability of the education system: What should the structure, content and objectives of secondary education be? How should teachers be trained for a modern secondary education? How should student learning be measured? What is the best way to manage a decentralized education system? How does information get produced and transmitted through the system to inform policy choices? Must the secondary system remain centralized or could regional solutions be managed? How much autonomy should schools have?

Demands for Greater Accountability. Civil society and governments are demanding that secondary education systems be accountable in a number of ways. People in the system need to be held accountable for accomplishing their assigned tasks, whether they are ministry staff, principals, teachers, parents, or students. The system should be accountable for ensuring students learn and for reporting to parents and the community on the status of that learning. In SSA, as pressure builds to ensure that children possess the skills they need to join the labor force, accountability mechanisms will extend beyond the high-stakes end-of-cycle examination results to other forms of student assessment and may well include such things as PTA reports on teacher attendance and reports on financial expenditures to the community. Clearly designated channels for public voice are essential for accountability, and government responsiveness to public opinion and demands will become increasingly important as the public has more, transparent information on which to judge education services.

Private-public Partnerships. Secondary education is a public good provided by governments and the private sector. Some parents pay for private secondary schools; others invest in private tutoring for their public school children; some private secondary schools receive government subsidies; vouchers allow some parents to take their taxes to the school of their choice. In SSA, secondary education is a public-private partnership. The balance of the partnership can change as demand for secondary education increases and as demands for equity change. Governments will become responsible for the accountability of private schools as they expand the provision of quality secondary education.

Governance of Secondary Education

> There is no single model of effective governance in secondary education [but there are] four common basic elements in countries that have a long tradition of state provision of . . . good secondary education: transparent, well-known regulations; a sharp definition of

responsibilities . . . of different levels of government; strong public management; precise definition of outcomes and measurement of results. (Ahmed 2000)

Governance must ensure that roles and responsibilities at different levels are aligned and communicated to avoid overlaps or gaps in responsibility and maximize coherence. Governance issues span all levels of an education system from the central ministry to the secondary school.

Public secondary education in SSA is not free or compulsory, and it certainly is not universal. Eligible students compete to move from small primary schools to large regional public secondary schools. The duration of secondary education varies across SSA, but usually totals seven years.[1] Secondary education may be general (academic) or vocational and typically prepares students either for tertiary education or the labor market. The academic and vocational tracks diverge, often after primary school, and do not reconverge. This stark separation contrasts with trends towards the convergence of general and vocational secondary education and training in other parts of the world (World Bank 2005).

There is no ideal configuration for a ministry of education. The tradition of highly centralized governments in SSA has concentrated governance functions in central ministries. The ongoing process of decentralization is distributing responsibilities slowly, but the local levels remain largely dependent on provincial or district education offices and have little autonomy. Responsibility for teacher training, deployment, and evaluation typically remains centralized in semi-autonomous government agencies, complicating local school management, and accountability.

Most SSA governments have set general goals for secondary schools, such as "producing productive citizens." To achieve this goal, they offer secondary education to a limited number of students made eligible through a high-stakes end-of-cycle examination, and allow the private sector to offer education to others. Education reforms in SSA might benefit from education reforms in other countries. In the early 20th century United States,

> the advent of a new economy . . . increased the demand for a small cadre of scientists and engineers, for a larger workforce of bureaucrats and public administrators . . . [and for] skilled and educated labor; in post-World War II Europe, the elitist secondary education system changed under the duress of international competition . . . ; East Asia, . . . Japan, Republic of Korea, Singapore, and Taiwan (China) adopted education policies to increase access and equity, concentrating on vocational education in upper secondary school . . . then shift[ing] to a more general curriculum. (Ahmed 2000)

The need for "producing such non-cognitive skills as creativity, spontaneity, flexibility and entrepreneurship, in great demand in the productive sector" has affected secondary education reforms worldwide (Ahmed 2000).

Governance Issues and Recommendations

- Secondary education policies need to clearly define the objectives of upper and lower, general and vocational secondary education. These definitions should lead

---

1. The mode of seven years in Africa is one of the highest of all regions: East Asia and the Pacific (6) Eastern Europe and Central Asia (7), LAC (5), the Middle East and North Africa (6), S. Asia (5), EU and US (6). See Table 1.3, Duration of Secondary Education Cycles by Region in Ahmed, 2000, p. 10.

to legislation and a regulatory framework that address the duration of secondary education, the pathways between general and vocational secondary education and between upper and lower secondary education, and ultimately on the relationship of secondary education and the labor market.
- All decisions concerning secondary education must be informed by data about the secondary education system's current performance. Without comprehensive, accurate data, policymaking can be unduly influenced by personal biases of ministers of education or senior civil servants, vested interests of school owners or teacher unions, and anecdotal evidence offered by business interests, journalists and politicians. Student performance data, if it is sufficiently detailed, can point to strengths and weaknesses in curriculum areas, show how intended curricula are implemented in schools, and highlight differences due to gender, rural-urban location, or performance at different times of the year. Such information could be used to improve curriculum design, teacher training, and the allocation of resources (Kellaghan and Greaney 2003).
- Effective education for the 21st century may require students to have a longer period of general education before specializing, clear pathways into and out of vocational training, and coordinated opportunities for school learning and apprenticeships in the labor force.
- The provision of information and communication technology in secondary schools is costly and requires a number of conditions that are not always satisfied (for example, stable supply of electricity, training, computer maintenance). Private-public partnerships are likely to provide some solutions to the need to incorporate such technology more effectively in secondary schools.
- Responsibility for secondary education is not always clearly designated in central ministries. This leads to confusion in provincial or district education offices and in schools about who is responsible for what, where, and when.
- The process of decentralization could leave central education ministries responsible for policy, planning and finance and give responsibility for management to regional offices, but to succeed, all levels of the hierarchy need to understand their responsibilities and be held accountable.
- The presence of a relatively autonomous teacher service commission tends to confuse lines of authority regarding teachers. If secondary school heads are expected to improve the quality of education in their schools, they need more leverage with respect to managing teachers.
- Private schools need to be regulated by SSA governments and held accountable for meeting the regulations.

Local Management of Secondary Education

Local management structures generally consist of a school's board of governors and parent-teacher association (PTA). Each of these bodies can have a significant impact on the quality of schooling offered, if they understand and embrace their roles. Unfortunately, many boards of governors are appointed and do not necessarily hold credentials in education. Many PTAs are recognized as entities that can supply funds to schools but are not given the voice they need to make a difference to the academic side of education. A secondary school head is responsible to each of these groups and serves as the school's central authority figure. He or she needs the mandate and management skills to oversee academic and financial tasks within the school and also needs the ability to present information to the local governing bodies in a manner that can persuade them to act in support of quality education.

Management Issues and Recommendations

- Management processes must clearly follow from educational objectives and specified lines of authority. The processes must help to avoid overlaps in responsibility and gaps in information.
- All staff must be informed and trained to carry out their roles and responsibilities.
- Management monitoring mechanisms must be defined and function. For example, the management processes that ensure that data circulates among the different education offices can act to inform and strengthen partnerships (central-local government, private-public) and ensure accountability.
- Clear procedures and the means to implement them must exist for the collection and transmission of school data through the levels of management so that information reaches the highest authorities and can serve as a basis for decisionmaking and policymaking.
- Selection of staff, including school leaders, should be based on competence rather than on seniority or political affiliation.

Accountability for Secondary Education

Accountability should exist at all levels of an education system. Ministry staff at all levels need to be accountable for meeting the requirements of their jobs; the education system should be accountable for educating students to a defined level of competency; and the system should be financially and academically accountable to parents and the community for doing its job. These three forms of accountability may be described as follows: *upward accountability* refers to the process of reporting to those above school management in the education hierarchy; *downward accountability* to an obligation that the school hierarchy has to learners, and *outward accountability* to the responsibility the school system has to community members. So, accountability pertains *to* all education providers *for* the education service that they provide *to* the public.

Accountability Issues and Recommendations

- Education systems need clearly defined reporting relationships, so all levels of the hierarchy know what information should be sent to what other parties on what schedule.
- Secondary education policy must have clear educational objectives and standards and include a mechanism for measuring whether student learning is meeting the standards. National assessments need to be introduced to provide relevant data about student learning.
- The roles of the inspector should be clearly defined, and the resources needed to effectively carry out those roles make available.

- Teacher accountability should be assessed by inspectors against clearly defined standards.
- Information management system must be put in place and used for decisionmaking through out the system.
- Defined, recognized channels must exist for the government to inform the public about education quality at every level, the progress of students, the policies under consideration, and the expenditure of funds. Parents and community members must receive the support they need to ensure that they can analyze the financial and academic information.
- Channels must also exist to allow the public to voice its opinions. Procedures must then be in place to ensure government responsiveness to public voice.

Private Secondary Schools

Because so much of secondary education in SSA is carried out by private institutions, it is critical that governments set education policies that apply to all secondary schools, include divisions within the ministry to govern private schools, and hold these schools accountable for meeting specified standards. However, when ministries are stretched to the limit with their attempts at accountability within the public system, private institutions often escape accountability.

Private School Issues and Recommendations

- Governments need to establish regulatory frameworks that facilitate the licensing and accountability of private schools to deliver quality education.
- Private schools must be monitored to ensure they are meeting the required standards.
- Mechanisms to encourage accountability should be designed, and could include making student assessment results public, aiding the creation of associations for private schools that may monitor their members, and creating participatory structures (for example, boards of governors or parent-teacher associations) for private secondary schools like those in public schools.

Résumé analytique

Objet de la présente étude

L'Initiative Éducation pour tous a conduit à un accroissement significatif du nombre d'écoliers qui terminent leurs études primaires en Afrique subsaharienne. Elle a également suscité une forte demande dans l'enseignement secondaire. La "voie royale" entre les études primaires et tertiaires fait face à de nombreux défis à relever à travers le monde. Conçu en grande partie dans les pays développés au XIXe siècle et au début du XXe siècle et transporté dans les pays en développement, l'enseignement secondaire n'est pas bien aligné sur les besoins et les objectifs du XXIe siècle. Les économies qui sont de plus en plus "axées sur le savoir" ont besoin de travailleurs ayant des connaissances étendues, des compétences développées et de plus en plus, la créativité et la souplesse d'un chef d'entreprise. Les gouvernements à travers le monde expérimentent différentes façons de baliser la voie de l'enseignement secondaire en itinéraires plus courts ou plus longs, avec un accent plus ou moins grand sur les volets académique ou professionnel, ainsi qu'une participation plus ou moins importante du secteur privé. Aucune solution ne prédomine pour la recherche d'un équilibre entre les exigences de cette économie axée sur le savoir et les préoccupations tout aussi légitimes concernant l'équité et les services de formation de grande qualité. Étant donné qu'un nombre croissant de personnes quittant l'école primaire cherchent à entrer dans l'enseignement secondaire, les pouvoirs publics des pays d'Afrique subsaharienne doivent évaluer les pratiques de gouvernance, de gestion et de responsabilisation dans leur enseignement secondaire, afin de s'assurer qu'ils sont en mesure de répondre aux besoins des élèves et de la société.

Définition des termes

Le terme *gouvernance* se définit de plusieurs manières dans les différentes études. Dans le présent rapport, ce terme traite de ce qui suit : i) la structure et la fonction de l'ensemble des systèmes d'enseignement secondaire, ii) le cadre législatif et réglementaire pour la fourniture de l'éducation et la gouvernance, iii) la structure, les rôles et les responsabilités des services centraux du ministère de l'Éducation et de ses organes décentralisés, et iv) les mécanismes de pilotage des établissements d'enseignement secondaire au niveau local (par exemple les conseils d'établissement et les associations des parents d'élèves et des enseignants). Le terme *gestion* porte sur les processus et les pratiques fixés par les lois et règlements ou par la pratique, aux fins d'atteindre les objectifs en matière d'éducation au niveau de l'établissement scolaire et de la communauté. La *responsabilisation* a trait aux processus par lesquels le système éducatif reconnaît lui-même qu'il est chargé de fournir des services de formation adaptés, et d'atteindre les objectifs qu'il s'est lui-même fixé en matière de formation des élèves.

Tendances ayant un impact sur l'enseignement secondaire en Afrique subsaharienne

Au niveau international, bon nombre de réformes dans l'enseignement secondaire découlent d'une inconciliabilité entre le système d'enseignement secondaire conçu lors de la révolution industrielle du XIXe siècle et les exigences technologiques du XXIe siècle. La demande croissante d'éducation et la pression pour plus d'accès, d'équité et de qualité induisent également des réformes dans le domaine de l'éducation. Ces pressions pour le changement affectent la gouvernance, la gestion et la responsabilisation dans l'enseignement secondaire. Les tendances au niveau international et leurs conséquences sur les pays d'Afrique subsaharienne peuvent se résumer ainsi qu'il suit :

Éducation pour tous (EPT) : Le programme Éducation pour tous avait eu un énorme impact sur l'enseignement secondaire : premièrement en faisant accroître la demande pour l'enseignement secondaire, et deuxièmement en se disputant les précieuses ressources qui sont indispensables à l'extension et à l'amélioration de la qualité du système d'enseignement secondaire.

Exigences de mondialisation. Dans un environnement qui se mondialise, le poste de travail exige des connaissances, des compétences techniques et des compétences en matière de résolution des problèmes et de capacité à analyser et à utiliser des informations dans la pratique. Il exige également des connaissances spécialisées dans le domaine des technologies de l'information et de la communication (TIC). Par conséquent, les ministères sont en train de revoir et de modifier les objectifs, la structure et les programmes de l'enseignement secondaire. Leur combat consiste à adapter un modèle industriel d'enseignement secondaire au monde moderne.

Davantage d'années de formation. À travers le monde, davantage de personnes suivent des études de plus en plus longues, et la durée de l'éducation de base obligatoire augmente. Le nombre d'années passées dans l'enseignement secondaire augmente également afin de s'adapter à l'explosion des nouvelles connaissances produites par des technologies qui se développent rapidement. Certains pouvoirs publics en Afrique subsaharienne élargissent l'accès à l'éducation de base gratuite, mais aucun d'entre eux ne propose la généralisation d'un enseignement secondaire gratuit. La demande de plus d'éducation a soulevé des questions concernant la gouvernance, la gestion et la responsabilisation du système éducatif : Que devrait être la structure, le contenu et les objectifs de l'enseignement secondaire ? Comment devraient être formés les enseignants pour un enseignement secondaire moderne ? Comment devrait être mesuré l'apprentissage par les élèves ? Quelle est la meilleure manière de gérer un système éducatif décentralisé ? Comment l'information est-elle produite et transmise par le biais du système afin d'étayer les choix de politique ? Le système de l'enseignement secondaire doit-il rester centralisé ou des solutions doivent-elles être envisagées au niveau régional ? Quel degré d'autonomie devraient avoir les établissements scolaires ?

Exigences d'une plus grande responsabilisation. La société civile et les pouvoirs publics demandent que les systèmes d'enseignement secondaire soient obligés de rendre compte de plusieurs manières. Les responsables du système doivent être tenus pour responsables de l'accomplissement des tâches assignées, qu'il s'agisse des employés du ministère, des chefs d'établissement scolaire, des enseignants, des parents ou des élèves. Le système doit être chargé de s'assurer que les élèves apprennent, et de présenter aux parents et à la communauté des rapports sur l'état d'avancement de cet apprentissage. En Afrique subsaharienne, au fur et à mesure que monte la pression pour s'assurer que les enfants possèdent les compétences techniques dont ils ont besoin pour rejoindre la population active, les mécanismes de responsabilisation s'étendront au-delà des résultats des examens de fin de cycle à grands enjeux, comparativement à d'autres formes d'évaluation des élèves. Parmi ces mécanismes, on peut citer les rapports des associations de parents d'élèves sur l'assiduité des enseignants et les rapports sur les dépenses budgétaires à présenter à la communauté. Des canaux clairement définis d'expression du public sont indispensables à la responsabilisation, et la réaction des gouvernants par rapport à l'opinion et aux exigences du public revêtira une importance de plus en plus grande si le public dispose d'une plus grande quantité d'informations transparentes à partir desquelles on peut apprécier les prestations dans le domaine de l'éducation.

Partenariats public/privé. L'enseignement secondaire est un bien public fourni par les pouvoirs publics et le secteur privé. Certains parents payent la scolarité dans les établissements d'enseignement secondaire privés ; d'autres investissent dans les leçons particulières pour leurs enfants des établissements scolaires publics ; quelques établissements privés d'enseignement secondaire bénéficient de subventions des pouvoirs publics ; des bons permettent à certains parents de payer l'équivalent de leurs impôts aux établissements de leur choix. En Afrique subsaharienne, l'enseignement secondaire est un partenariat entre le secteur public et le secteur privé. Dans ce partenariat, l'équilibre peut se modifier si la demande d'enseignement secondaire augmente et si les exigences d'équité se modifient. Les pouvoirs publics deviendront responsables de l'obligation des établissements privés de rendre compte au fur et à mesure qu'ils fournissent de plus en plus un enseignement secondaire de qualité.

Gouvernance dans l'enseignement secondaire

> Il n'existe pas un modèle unique de gouvernance efficace dans l'enseignement secondaire [mais on compte] quatre éléments fondamentaux courants dans les pays ayant une longue tradition de fourniture par l'État ... d'un bon enseignement secondaire ; d'une réglementation transparente et bien connue de tous ; une définition précise des responsabilités... à différents niveaux de l'administration publique ; gestion publique saine ; définition précise des réalisations et mesure des résultats. (Ahmed 2000)

La gouvernance doit veiller à ce que les rôles et les responsabilités à différents niveaux soient alignés et communiqués afin non seulement d'éviter des chevauchements et des déficits de responsabilités, mais également de maximiser la cohérence. Les questions de gouvernance couvrent tous les niveaux d'un système éducatif, des services centraux du ministère à l'établissement d'enseignement secondaire.

En Afrique subsaharienne, l'enseignement secondaire public n'est ni gratuit ni obligatoire ; et il n'est certainement pas accessible à tous. Les élèves éligibles sont en concurrence pour passer des petits établissements d'enseignement primaire aux grands établissements d'enseignement secondaire au niveau régional. En Afrique subsaharienne, la durée de l'enseignement secondaire varie d'un pays à l'autre, mais elle est souvent de sept ans en tout[1]. L'enseignement secondaire peut être général (académique) ou professionnel ; il prépare généralement les élèves soit pour le tertiaire, soit pour le marché du travail. Les pistes académiques et professionnelles divergent très souvent après l'école primaire et n'ont pas de point de convergence plus tard. Cette profonde séparation contraste avec les tendances vers la convergence de l'enseignement secondaire général et professionnel et la formation dans d'autres parties du monde (Banque mondiale 2005).

Il n'existe pas de configuration idéale pour un ministère de l'Éducation. La tradition des gouvernements très centralisés en Afrique subsaharienne a concentré les fonctions de gouvernance dans les services centraux des ministères. Le processus de décentralisation en cours distribue les responsabilités lentement, mais le niveau local demeure largement dépendant des délégations provinciales ou départementales de l'Éducation, et bénéficie ainsi de peu d'autonomie. La responsabilité de la formation, du déploiement et de l'évaluation des enseignants demeure généralement centralisée dans les organismes publics semi autonomes, ce qui complique la gestion des établissements scolaires et la responsabilisation des dirigeants au niveau local.

La plupart des gouvernements d'Afrique subsaharienne ont fixé des objectifs généraux que doivent réaliser les établissements d'enseignement secondaire, tels que « la formation de citoyens productifs. » Pour réaliser cet objectif, les pouvoirs publics proposent un enseignement secondaire à un nombre limité d'élèves devenus éligibles par le biais d'un examen de fin de cycle à grands enjeux, et permettent au secteur privé de dispenser la formation aux autres. Les réformes de l'éducation en Afrique subsaharienne pourraient tirer avantage des réformes en matière d'éducation qui sont mises en place dans d'autres pays. Aux États-Unis du début du XXe siècle,

> l'avènement d'une nouvelle économie... a augmenté la demande d'un petit cadre de scientifiques et d'ingénieurs, pour un plus grand effectif de bureaucrates et d'administrateurs civils... [et pour] des travailleurs qualifiés et instruits ; dans l'Europe d'après la Deuxième guerre mondiale, le système élitiste d'enseignement secondaire a connu des modifications sous la contrainte de la concurrence internationale... ; en Asie de l'Est, ... le Japon, la République de Corée, Singapour et Taiwan (Chine) ont adopté des politiques éducatives visant à accroître l'accès et l'équité, en se concentrant sur la formation professionnelle dans les établissements d'enseignement secondaire du second cycle ... et en se tournant ensuite vers un programme d'études plus général. (Ahmed 2000)

Le besoin de « produire des compétences non cognitives du type créativité, spontanéité, souplesse et esprit d'entreprise, qui sont très demandés dans le secteur productif » (Ahmed 2000) a eu un impact sur les réformes de l'enseignement secondaire à travers le monde.

Questions liées à la gouvernance et recommandations

- Les politiques d'enseignement secondaire doivent définir clairement les objectifs du premier cycle et du second cycle de l'enseignement secondaire général et profes-

---

1. Sept ans en Afrique figure parmi les durées les plus longues par rapport aux autres régions : Asie de l'Est et Pacifique (6), Europe de l'Est et Asie centrale (7), Moyen-Orient et Afrique du Nord (6), Asie du Sud (5), Union européenne et États-Unis (6). Voir le Tableau 1.3, *Duration of Secondary Education Cycles by Region*, Ahmed, 2000, p. 10.

sionnel. Ces définitions doivent donner lieu à un cadre législatif et réglementaire qui traite de la durée de l'enseignement secondaire, de la passerelle entre l'enseignement secondaire général et professionnel et entre le premier cycle et le second cycle de l'enseignement secondaire, et en fin de compte des rapports entre l'enseignement secondaire et le marché du travail.

- Toutes les décisions concernant l'enseignement secondaire doivent être étayées par des données sur la performance actuelle du système d'enseignement secondaire. En l'absence de données exhaustives et exactes, la prise de décision peut être indûment influencée par les partis pris des ministres de l'Éducation ou des hauts fonctionnaires, les droits acquis des propriétaires d'établissements ou des associations d'enseignants, et les preuves anecdotiques fournies par les entreprises commerciales, les journalistes et les hommes politiques. Si elles sont suffisamment détaillées, les données sur la performance des élèves peuvent indiquer les points forts et les points faibles des programmes d'études, montrer comment les programmes d'études envisagés sont mis en œuvre dans les établissements scolaires, et mettre en lumière les différences dues aux inégalités entre les sexes, à l'implantation des établissements en milieu rural ou urbain, ou aux performances au cours des différentes périodes de l'année. Ces informations pourraient être utilisées pour améliorer l'élaboration des programmes d'études, la formation des enseignants et l'affectation des ressources (Kellaghan and Greaney 2003).
- Au XXIe siècle, une éducation efficace peut exiger que les élèves aient une plus longue période d'enseignement général avant de se spécialiser, qu'il y ait des passerelles clairement définies pour s'engager dans la formation professionnelle ou en sortir, et qu'il existe des occasions coordonnées de formation scolaire et d'apprentissage au sein de la population active.
- La fourniture des technologies de l'information et de la communication aux établissements secondaires est coûteuse et requiert un certain nombre de conditions qui ne sont pas toujours réunies (par exemple, la permanence de la fourniture d'électricité, la formation, la maintenance informatique). Il est indispensable que les partenariats entre le secteur public et le secteur privé apportent des solutions au besoin d'introduire cette technologie de manière plus efficace dans les établissements secondaires.
- Dans les services centraux des ministères, on ne sait toujours pas de manière claire qui est responsable de l'enseignement secondaire. Cette situation aboutit à la confusion dans les délégations provinciales et départementales de l'éducation et dans les établissements scolaires au sujet de qui est chargé de quoi, où et quand.
- Le processus de décentralisation peut permettre de laisser aux services centraux des ministères la charge de la politique, de la planification et des finances, et confier la responsabilité de la gestion aux délégations régionales. Mais pour réussir, tous les niveaux de la hiérarchie doivent bien connaître leurs responsabilités et être responsabilisés.
- La présence d'une commission relativement autonome chargée du service des enseignants tend à rendre confuse la voie hiérarchique concernant les enseignants. Si l'on veut que les chefs d'établissements scolaires améliorent la qualité de la formation dans leurs établissements, ils doivent avoir plus de pouvoirs en ce qui concerne la gestion des enseignants.

- Les établissements privés doivent respecter les prescriptions des pouvoirs publics et être responsabilisés par rapport au respect de la réglementation.

Gestion de l'enseignement secondaire au niveau local

Les structures de gestion au niveau local comprennent généralement un conseil d'établissement et une association des parents d'élèves (APE). Chacun de ces organes peut avoir une grande influence bénéfique sur la qualité de la formation offerte si chacun connaît bien et joue son rôle. Malheureusement, bon nombre de membres de conseils d'établissement sont nommés et ne sont pas nécessairement titulaires de diplômes en éducation. Plusieurs APE sont reconnues comme des entités pouvant fournir des fonds aux établissements, mais on ne leur permet pas de faire entendre un son de cloche différent quand il s'agit des questions académiques. Un chef d'établissement secondaire est responsable devant chacun de ces groupes et joue le rôle d'autorité centrale au sein de l'établissement. Il ou elle a besoin d'un mandat et des compétences en gestion pour superviser les tâches d'ordre académique ou financier au sein de l'établissement. Il a également besoin de l'aptitude à présenter l'information aux conseils d'administration locaux d'une manière pouvant les persuader de prendre des mesures en faveur d'une éducation de qualité.

Problèmes de gestion et recommandations

- Les processus de gestion doivent suivre de manière claire les objectifs éducatifs et respecter les voies hiérarchiques prévues. Ces processus doivent permettre d'éviter les chevauchements de responsabilité et les déficits d'information.
- Tout le personnel doit être informé et formé pour jouer son rôle et assumer ses responsabilités.
- Des mécanismes de suivi de la gestion doivent être définis et fonctionner. À titre d'exemple, les processus de gestion qui font en sorte que les données circulent entre les différentes délégations de l'éducation peuvent être mis en place afin d'enrichir et de renforcer les partenariats (administration centrale/locale, secteur public/privé), et de permettre la responsabilisation.
- Il doit exister des procédures claires et les moyens de les mettre en oeuvre en vue de la collecte et de la transmission des données sur les établissements scolaires à travers les systèmes de gestion, de telle sorte que l'information parvienne aux plus hautes autorités et puisse servir de base à la prise de décision et à l'élaboration de la politique.
- Le choix du personnel, y compris les dirigeants d'établissements scolaires, devrait reposer sur la compétence et non sur l'ancienneté ou l'appartenance politique.

Responsabilisation dans l'enseignement secondaire

La responsabilisation devrait exister à tous les niveaux d'un système éducatif. Les employés du ministère à tous les niveaux doivent être responsables du respect des exigences de leurs postes ; le système éducatif doit avoir l'obligation de rendre compte de la formation des élèves à un niveau précis de compétence ; et le système devrait être financièrement et académiquement responsable devant les parents et à la communauté. Ces trois formes de responsabilisation peuvent être décrites de la manière suivante : la « responsabilisation vers le haut » porte sur le processus consistant à rendre compte aux supérieurs de la direction de l'établissement dans la hiérarchie éducative ; la « responsabilisation vers le bas » a trait à l'obligation que la hiérarchie de l'établissement a vis-à-vis des élèves, et la « responsabilisation vers l'extérieur » vise la responsabilité que le système scolaire a vis-à-vis des membres de la communauté. Ainsi donc, la responsabilisation concerne tous les prestataires de services éducatifs qui sont fournis au public.

Questions liées à la responsabilisation et recommandations

- Les systèmes éducatifs nécessitent des relations bien définies en matière de production de rapports, de telle sorte que tous les niveaux de la hiérarchie aient connaissance de l'information à transmettre aux autres parties en fonction d'un calendrier.
- La politique d'enseignement secondaire doit fixer des normes et des objectifs éducatifs clairs et comprendre un mécanisme permettant de savoir si la formation des élèves respecte les normes. Des évaluations au niveau national doivent être introduites afin de fournir des données pertinentes concernant l'apprentissage par les élèves.
- Les rôles que doit jouer l'inspecteur doivent être clairement définis, et les ressources indispensables pour jouer efficacement ces rôles doivent être disponibles.
- Les inspecteurs devraient évaluer la responsabilité des enseignants par rapport aux normes clairement définies.
- Un système de gestion de l'information doit être mis en place et utilisé pour la prise de décision d'un bout à l'autre du système.
- Il est indispensable que des canaux définis et acceptés existent afin que le public soit informé de la qualité de la formation à chaque niveau, des progrès réalisés par les élèves, des politiques envisagées et des fonds dépensés. Les parents et les membres de la communauté doivent bénéficier du soutien dont ils ont besoin pour s'assurer qu'ils soient capables d'analyser les informations financières et académiques.
- Il doit également exister des canaux permettant au public de donner son avis. Il faut donc mettre en place des procédures visant à garantir la réaction des pouvoirs publics par rapport aux avis donnés par le public.

Établissements privés d'enseignement secondaire

Étant donné qu'une grande partie de l'enseignement secondaire en Afrique subsaharienne est dispensée par des établissements privés, il est important que les pouvoirs publics élaborent des politiques éducatives qui s'appliquent à tous les établissements d'enseignement secondaire, impliquent les directions du ministère dans l'administration des établissements privés et rendent ces établissement responsables du respect des normes prescrites. Cependant, lorsque les ministères sont poussés jusqu'à l'extrême en ce qui concerne leurs tentatives de responsabilisation au sein du système public, les établissements privés échappent souvent à la responsabilisation.

Problèmes de l'enseignement privé et recommandations

- Les pouvoirs publics ont besoin de mettre en place des cadres réglementaires qui facilitent l'octroi des autorisations d'ouverture et la responsabilisation des établissements privés en vue de la fourniture d'une éducation de qualité.
- Les établissements privés doivent bénéficier d'un suivi afin de s'assurer qu'ils respectent les normes requises.
- Des mécanismes visant à encourager l'obligation de rendre compte devraient être conçus, notamment en publiant les résultats des évaluations des élèves, en aidant à la création d'associations des établissements privés qui peuvent assurer le suivi de leurs membres, et en mettant en place dans les établissements privés d'enseignement secondaire des structures participatives (par exemple les conseils d'établissement et les associations de parents d'élèves et d'enseignants) semblables à celles qui existent dans les établissements publics.

CHAPTER 1

Introduction

This study was undertaken for the World Bank's Secondary Education in Africa (SEIA) initiative by the American Institutes for Research (AIR). The study was designed jointly by AIR and Khulisa Management Services in South Africa. AIR developed the literature review and data collection protocols and completed the desk review of Uganda secondary education. Khulisa Management Services supervised the work of researchers in three Sub-Saharan African countries (Senegal, South Africa, and Zambia) who carried out interviews and collected information from a variety of sources to develop the case studies. AIR, in consultation with the World Bank SEIA team and other advisors, finalized the report.

The AIR team was led by Dr. Deborah Glassman with support from Dr. Jane Benbow and drew on many colleagues from ministries, schools and AIR projects in Sub-Saharan Africa. Pat Sullivan and Khulisa Management Services oversaw the team responsible for the field research for the three case studies.

Purpose of This Study

Education for All (EFA) has led to a significant increase in the number of students completing primary education in Sub-Saharan Africa (SSA). It has also created tremendous demand for secondary education and has therefore pushed forward the need for Sub-Saharan governments to find effective ways of responding to these demands. The "highway" between primary and tertiary education faces challenges on many levels, not only in SSA. The model and objectives of secondary education largely adhered to in SSA were developed for 19th and early 20th centuries western societies. That model has remained fundamentally unchanged, especially in developing countries which struggle to align secondary education with the market needs of the 21st century. Awareness is growing worldwide that secondary education must provide students with the knowledge, skills and competencies that make them productive in economies that are increasingly "knowledge-driven," preparing them for both tertiary education and for the labor market. Consequently, governments worldwide are experimenting with different ways of tracing and dividing the secondary highway into shorter or longer routes, with a more or less general academic or vocational emphasis or a synthesis of the two, with more or less involvement from the private sector, and with more or less concern for equipping students with skills for the knowledge economy. Balancing these imperatives with a concern for equity and for the quality of education is not easy, and no single solution will prevail.

As SSA governments seek to ensure that more primary school leavers make the transition to secondary education, they must evaluate their secondary education systems, with a particular look at how they are governed, managed and held accountable. To strengthen them, they must be prepared to undertake coherent, systemic changes. This study, part of the examination of secondary education in SSA, seeks to provide useful input into such decisions about changes.

This report is part of the World Bank SEIA project, which is designed to collect and summarize information on best practices and identify sustainable development plans for expansion and improved quality, equity and efficiency in the delivery of secondary education in SSA. As one of several thematic studies for the SEIA project, this report focuses on governance, management, and accountability in secondary education.

Definition of Terms and Scope of the Report

In this section, we define how this paper addresses governance, management, accountability within secondary education systems in SSA. It is important to clarify how this paper will approach each of these concepts because separating and pulling them apart for analysis is not an easy task. Good governance, management and accountability are an interdependent set of relationships; each depends on the quality of the other for the effective functioning of the system as a whole Governance can not be good governance without systems of accountability. The same is true for management systems—they must have points of action and systems for holding management accountable. No system established for governance can function without processes and structures for its management. This report therefore draws somewhat artificial lines among the three concepts and how it examines each of those concepts within the framework of this report.

Finally, this definition of terms briefly discusses decentralization as it is so critical to the context in which governance, management and accountability function throughout Sub-Saharan Africa.

Governance

World Bank publications have defined governance as ". . . the manner in which power is exercised in the management of a country's economic and social development" (World Bank 1994). In other discussions, governance is defined as the means by which an activity or a sample of activities is controlled and directed (Glatter 2005). "Good governance is epitomized by predictable, open and enlightened policymaking, a bureaucracy imbued with a professional ethos acting in furtherance of the public good, the rule of law, transparent processes, and a strong civil society participating in public affairs" (Kruiter 1995). Regarding the topic of this paper, "There is no explicit agreement on how to define education governance." There is an implicit assumption, however, that governance refers to the "machinery of government—that is, what the ministry of education and education offices do . . ." (World Bank 2005).

In the developed world, "(t)here is no single model of effective governance in secondary education" that might be taken as a model for SSA, "(but there are) four common basic elements in countries that have a long tradition of state provision of compulsory secondary education and . . . reasonable success in providing most . . . young people with good secondary education" (World Bank 2002).

These include "transparent, well-known regulations; a sharp definition of responsibilities . . . of different levels of government; strong public management; precise definition of outcomes and measurement of results" (World Bank 2005).

Governance must ensure that roles and responsibilities at different levels be aligned or at least coordinated and communicated to avoid overlaps or gaps in responsibility and maximize coherence. There are many dimensions to education governance, which spans all levels of an education system (World Bank 2005). Selecting from these definitions, the discussion of governance in this report focuses on three major topics: How secondary education is defined and structured in selected countries of SSA, what the major policies shaping the vision for the objectives, governance system, and provision of secondary education in selected SSA countries, and the organization and distribution of roles and responsibilities in the central ministry and decentralized offices located in districts or provincial capitals. Insofar as the data has permitted it, we distinguish between upper and lower secondary education in our discussion.

In this report, governance does not include local structures of school governance; these are instead addressed under "management." In consequence, management refers to the processes by which local staff—educators in schools and community members in boards of governors and parent-teacher associations—fulfill the roles and responsibilities laid out in policy and legislation. Clearly, if a governance structure is vague or is missing certain elements, it is very difficult for management to function well. If managers are not competent or trained, do not understand their roles, or work under conditions that do not enable them to carry out their responsibilities, no matter how well defined the governance structure is, it cannot function as intended. In practice, then, governance and management are intertwined, even at the local level.

Similarly, governance and accountability often overlap. As cited above, governance includes a "definition of outcomes and a measurement of results." Within this paper, we are considering these as a part of accountability. So, accountability includes the mechanisms used by a ministry to assess the success of its educational system and issue sanctions if expectations are not met. Schools may be held accountable for the safety of their facilities, the conduct of their teachers, and the learning of their students. Of course, it is difficult to separate accountability from governance and management, as neither the governance structure nor management procedures work well without accountability mechanisms, which ensure that there is some measure of how well the system works, and some feedback which leads to changes in governance and management if the system does not work well.

Management

Management is often defined quite broadly as the processes and practices designed to realize objectives at all levels of the education system: who carries out what responsibilities, how the various parts of the system communicate with each other, and how 'checks and balances' work among the levels. In theory, education management includes staff in the central ministry, satellite ministry offices at the provincial and district levels, secondary and vocational school, and in school governing boards and parent-teacher associations. However, within this paper, we specifically address what happens at the local level, leaving ministry management for another day. In its focus on the local level, this paper discusses the responsibilities of secondary school heads, along with their boards of governors and parent-teacher associations.

Accountability

> Accountability refers to holding the providers of services answerable to the beneficiaries and other stakeholders regarding both process and outcome of a program. Openness and transparency in management and a participatory approach in planning, making key decisions, and evaluation are necessary conditions of accountability. (Ahmed 2000)

Accountability is a transitive activity: someone is accountable to someone else for something. Governments are accountable to their citizens for delivering public goods and services, including education. Accountability in an education system (USAID 2004) refers to the complex interplay between the service providers and the users, which include students, parents and the broader community. The entire governance and management system from policymakers (Heads of State, ministry officials at all levels, experts) to teachers, from mid-level staff to school leaders can be considered service providers who are accountable.

Accountability has three dimensions. First, education staff is accountable to those in the educational hierarchy above them. School principals must demonstrate to district or provincial education office staff that they are doing their jobs, and they must also show their local board of governors and parent-teacher association that the school is meeting requirements. Similarly, teachers must demonstrate their competence to their principals. Second, educators and education managers are accountable to students who come to the institution with a desire to learn. Educators are obliged to deliver a program of studies that meets students' needs. Third, the education system is accountable to parents and the community. These adults pay fees for children to be educated, and they should be presented with evidence that learning has occurred, as advertised. They need access to meaningful information and a voice in school management.

Accountability must be addressed as a part of the description of governance, and it must be managed carefully. To function, the accountability system must have a specified chain of command, clearly assigned responsibilities for activities, a mechanism to redress errors, and consequences for failure to meet requirements.

This paper discusses the processes that support upward and downward accountability in the secondary education system and processes designed to ensure internal accountability and accountability for learning outcomes.

Decentralization: The Context of Governance, Management and Accountability

Decentralization is the process whereby a central government assigns roles and responsibilities to lower, more local levels of the system. Since the 1960s, governments world wide have been decentralizing authority and finances; today the vast majority of developing countries are also engaged in efforts to decentralize. Degrees of decentralization vary as a function of how much responsibility for decisionmaking and finance are assigned to each administrative level. International experience within the education sector reveals a wide variation in decentralization designs, ranging from transfers from central to sub-national levels to investing significant authority and responsibilities in schools and local parent-based bodies.

Box 1. Decentralization

"For decentralized management to effectively support school improvement, changes in responsibility and administrative behavior are required throughout the system. There is a need for an institutional framework for the delivery of education based on empowering communities and officials to participate in educational management to support quality education provision and outcomes. This does not mean a minimal role for central, regional, or local educational administration structures but rather a changed role for different levels and actors. Central governments retain authority over policymaking, financing of education, national curriculum, and overall quality assurance, while passing on day-to-day administrative and management responsibilities to regional, district or school levels to develop and support educational changes. International experience reveals a wide variation in decentralization designs, ranging from transfers from central to sub-national levels as well as to school level . . . [It] varies from giving school councils or governing bodies limited authority to allocate non-personnel budgets to allowing autonomy under strict performance contracts to almost complete management autonomy."

Source: Winkler (2005).

Virtually all SSA governments have decentralized some responsibility for secondary education, but they have done so to different degrees.[2] The question is whether the degree of decentralization is accompanied by the conditions that enable it to work effectively. Are roles and responsibilities defined at every level? Are competent staff hired to fill positions? Are staff trained to take on their jobs? Has the governance structure avoided overlaps or gaps of responsibility and authority to avoid confusion? Is data created, collected, and transmitted efficiently through the decentralized offices to ensure that decisions can be made based on reliable, transparent information? The examples of governance structures discussed below are decentralized to different degrees; the issue is not whether their arrangements are theoretically ideal, but whether the necessary conditions exist to make the arrangement effective.

---

2. Winkler and Herschberg differentiate degrees of decentralization of administrative, fiscal and political responsibility as deconcentration to regional offices, devolution to regional offices or local administrations, and delegation to schools and/or communities.

The process of decentralization that SSA countries are undergoing affects all of the topics addressed in this paper: The kinds of policies that will be most effective, how power and responsibility to different level of it structure should be assigned, what management structures are most appropriate, and what mechanisms should be used to assure accountability.

Private schools pose special governance, and accountability challenges, which are addressed in this report to the extent that data is available. The use of information and communication technologies constitutes an area of special concern, as ICT is an intrinsic part of the modern world, a necessary tool and a significant element in the globalizing knowledge economy. This report therefore discusses some of the issues related to ICT and its impact on secondary education systems in SSA.

To explore the issues discussed about this report is organized as follows:

- Chapter 2 examines international trends in secondary education and how they are affecting SSA governments as they manage their secondary education systems.
- Chapters 3 addresses governance, including the structure of upper and lower secondary education in SSA, the policies of selected SSA Ministries of Education and the distributions of roles and responsibilities at different levels of decentralized management.
- Chapter 4 addresses management, focusing on school-level management as the place where governance structures and management processes converge. It examines the role of various governance structures for secondary schools and their impact on the management of teachers and of general academic and financial management.
- Chapter 5 focuses on accountability and explores its upward, downward, and outward forms. It summarizes the ways both student learning and the general performance of secondary education are currently assessed in SSA.
- Chapter 6 addresses the particular issues involved in the governance and accountability of private schools, including their regulation, licensing, and financing.
- Chapter 7 provides a brief discussion of ICT issues as they effective secondary education.
- The final chapter summarizes the discussions in terms of the key issues and suggestions for improvements within educational governance, management, and accountability.

The body of published literature from SSA on governance, management, and accountability in secondary education is still in its infancy. Therefore, this paper has drawn on literature concerning the concepts of governance, management and accountability in general and pertinent parts of the copious literature on school governance and management from North America, Latin and South America, Europe, and Asia. It has also drawn extensively on interviews with actors at different levels of education systems in selected SSA countries to give a voice to the actors on the ground.

CHAPTER 2

International Trends Influencing Secondary Education in Sub-Saharan Africa

Before beginning our discussion of governance, management, and accountability of secondary education in SSA, it is important to know something of the broader context within which this discussion is taking place. The international trends discussed below are driving much of the need for reform in secondary education through out the SSA region.

Education for All (EFA): The international commitment to basic education for all and free universal primary education that coalesced around the 1990 Jomtiem and the 2000 Darkar meeting has driven the policies and financial investments of donors and developing nations alike. The successes of this international movement have addressed many of the equity and quality issues facing developing countries as they expand their educational systems. EFA has thus drastically increased the demand from secondary education while competing with the resources necessary to respond to that demand.

More Education: Completing Secondary Becomes the Norm in Developing Countries

In almost all OECD countries the level of educational attainment is on the rise, "on average, three-quarters of people born in the 1970's have gone all the way through secondary school" (OECD 2005). Secondary schooling is now an essential requirement of successful entry into the labor market.

More Compulsory Education

Longer periods of compulsory education are becoming a worldwide norm. Lower secondary education is almost universally compulsory in Asia, North America, Europe, and Australasia.

Some SSA countries are extending basic compulsory education. In Mali, basic education is going from six to nine years, in Kenya, Senegal, and Zambia, basic education lasts for eight years.[3] Longer basic education allows more time for the consolidation of learning (Holsinger and Cowell 2000).

More Youth Complete Upper Secondary

The OECD Education Indicators 2005 show that in almost all OECD countries, the proportion of individuals finishing upper secondary education is growing, often rapidly. In 22 countries, the proportion of the youngest generation now in school ranges from 71 percent to 97 percent. "Many countries with traditionally low levels of education are catching up, and completion of upper secondary almost everywhere has become the norm for youth cohorts" (OECD 2005). The situation is less dynamic in SSA, but the trend is already apparent in lower secondary, where the crush of demand from primary completers is making itself felt. The private market has been able to respond more quickly to this demand than the public education system.

Transition to a Global Economy

Secondary education worldwide is struggling to accommodate itself to changing needs in a globalizing world and workplace. Employers in the developed world seek employees with knowledge, skills, and the ability to solve problems, and may measure these through assessments. For employers, educators, and the public, the emphasis has shifted from education inputs to education outcomes. International assessments such as the Programme for International Student Assessment (PISA) reflect this shift from testing curriculum-based learning to testing for pragmatic problem-solving. PISA tests 15-year-old students in many different developed countries on their capacity to solve math, reading, and science problems of the sort that they meet in daily life and will confront in a knowledge economy. The Trends in International Mathematics and Science Study (TIMSS) tests knowledge and problem-solving in just two disciplines allowing for outcome comparisons within and across countries. South Africa is the only country in southern or central Africa to have participated in these assessments. The assessments carried out by the Southern and Eastern Africa Consortium for Monitoring Educational Quality (SACMEQ) are of the educational quality of basic, not secondary education.[4]

ICT, Employment, and Education

Technology is virtually ubiquitous in the workplace in the developed world. Its use is measured in various studies which show, for example, that in Europe, "ICT-skilled employment has generally increased in EU15 countries" (OECD 2004). In Japan, slightly more

---

3. See Appendix B regarding duration of lower and upper secondary education.
4. SACMEQ 1 tested reading and then mathematics for 6th graders. Participant education ministries included Kenya, Malawi, Mauritius, Namibia, Tanzania (Zanzibar), Zambia, and Zimbabwe. SACMEQ II participants included Botswana, Kenya, Lesotho, Malawi, Mauritius, Mozambique, Namibia, Seychelles, South Africa, Swaziland, Tanzania (Mainland and Zanzibar), Uganda, and Zambia.

than 60 percent of jobs in information and research services employ people with ICT skills. This may be unsurprising, but it points to the connection between information and technology and the need for an ICT-skilled labor force to improve the production of information and knowledge. In the United States, over 30 percent of people working in lumber and building material retailing, for example, use ICT (OECD 2004).

The big question is how to link the need for ICT skills in the workplace with appropriate education, especially when ICT itself is changing quickly and changing what we know very quickly.

> Countries can use education policies to ensure that skills needs are satisfied in the long run. However, precisely because they are effective in the long term, they may not be appropriate for supplying specific (and advanced) ICT skills needs, which may change rapidly . . . While it can be argued that education can satisfy at least basic needs . . . large investments in computer skills and educational programmes in order to teacher pupils how to use computers are likely to be ineffective . . . (OECD 2004)

Greater Accountability

Focus on School Leadership

Box 2. Decentralization to Schools

"One type of education reform has been gaining support in developing countries in the past decade. It is transforming the way public schools operate, making them more directly accountable to students, parents, and communities. This reform is known by several names—school-based management, school autonomy reform, school improvement programs—but is (sic) really different forms of administrative decentralization."

Source: King and Ozler (1998), p. 1.3

The school, as the most local education unit, has become a locus of demand for accountability. School principals, as leaders of their schools, are charged with making their school perform. The reforms that focus on the school and school leadership go by at least two names: Comprehensive School Reform (CRS) or whole-school reform seeks to overhaul the school system by aligning policies and practices with a coherent central vision, an approach that grew out of the US Congressional Comprehensive School Reform Demonstration program to improve public primary and secondary education; Shared Decision-Making (SDM) approaches to school reform aim to empower teachers (Coffey and Lashway 2001).

Standards-driven Accountability

Another general demand is that education systems produce educated students that meet established standards. Such a demand requires that education standards be defined along with a mechanism for regularly assessing whether students are learning all that is required. By measuring what pupils learn and then comparing what they learn to what they are supposed to learn at specific education levels, the quality of education in a particular school or across the entire secondary education system can be judged more effectively than by the use of high-stakes end-of-year examinations. Standards-driven accountability is "without question, the dominant state-level strategy today.... [E]xplicit performance standards, systematic testing, and consequences for results . . . will stimulate teachers and students to focus their efforts in the right direction" (Coffey and Lashway 2001). Standards-driven accountability also facilitates international comparisons, which adds another dimension of accountability at the highest levels of governments to their populations.[5]

Diversified Providers: Public Private Partnerships

Education has historically been a private/public partnership, with varying degrees of responsibility for different providers at different points in time; the church was replaced by government as the main provider of education in Europe and SSA, but it remains an important education provider in SSA particularly. Dissatisfaction with public schools fuels the private market worldwide. In the United States, vouchers reflect a demand for greater school choice; in secular France, the government subsidizes church-run schools and provides teachers for private schools; in SSA, the church continues to be a major education provider. As SSA governments modernize their provision of secondary education, their relationships with private providers will be essential and require both more regulation and greater creativity in finding points of leverage to ensure cooperation. Of course, dependence on a private sector to provide education raises questions of equity: if ability to pay is a major criterion for getting an education, how will SSA governments square their need for a trained labor force with demands for equity?

Complicating the international reforms in secondary education is an incompatibility between a secondary education system developed in the 19th century and one that can meet 21st century demands. Educational reform in Europe in 19th century and in the United States in the early 20th where geared to "the advent of a new economy . . . increased the demand for a small cadre of scientists and engineers, for a larger workforce of bureaucrats and public administrators, and, most significantly, for skilled and educated labor. In 1900, there emerged in the United States the notion that schooling could make ordinary office clerks, shop floor workers, and even farmers more productive" (World Bank 2005).

A key element that has served the system well up to the present day especially in the American system was the training of an intelligent professional corps of educators—professionals with a shared vision for what secondary education should be. These professional educators represented a new class of reformers who had been trained in the "science" of education, organizational management, assessment, and so forth. They worked to standardize practice in secondary schools, to wrest the schools out of the control of local, parochial school boards (which oversaw a chaotic curriculum) and to "regularize" what was taught and how. These professional educators advocated structures and curricula based on principles of best practice in the field rather than on nepotism or local biases. One critical

---

5. PISA, TIMSS, and OECD indicators are well-known international examples.

component in reform was the creation of new schools of education where teachers and administrators learned standard ideas about structure, assessment and governance.

In Africa, however, the development of a secondary education system was based on the structures and practices of their colonial rulers with one very important distinction. These system were not designed to meet the developing economies of the people and context to which where transported. They were instead designed to produce the kind of labor power needed to support and expand colonial rule. Nevertheless the systems have become entrenched and any reform effort will struggle with how to adapt as well as change these systems.

CHAPTER 3

Issues of Governance in Secondary Education in Sub-Saharan Africa

"In most of Anglophone Sub-Saharan Africa, the pattern of 25 years of neglect of secondary education is to be found." There are exceptions, as in smaller, richer Botswana, and *"in countries like Ghana and Zambia, where the break between primary and secondary has been blurred by the attempt to stretch the duration of a common basic education."*

—phone conversation with Terry Allsop

At a minimum, the concept of governance of secondary education begins by understanding the structure and functions of the system; the education vision and legislation which guides the system's structure, content, objectives, funding, and access; and the roles and responsibilities of the staff in the offices that support those functions and objectives at all levels.

There is no ideal configuration for an education ministry or for its decentralized offices. In SSA, the tradition of highly centralized governments has tended to concentrate authority in central ministries. The process of decentralization is distributing these responsibilities differently; over the last decade there has movement towards locating responsibilities for planning and policy at the central level and moving management functions to regional levels (for example, Botswana and Senegal). Whatever the degree of decentralization, some conditions are critical for effective governance: i) the assignment of responsibilities and authority should be clear and avoid overlap and gaps; and ii) staff should be selected or elected on the basis of demonstrated competence and be trained for specific job responsibilities. As discussed later in the paper, it is also important that these staff have access to reliable data to use for decisionmaking; and that they be held accountable for accomplishing their given tasks. Thus, governance embraces and cannot be totally separated from management, or from accountability.

Bearing these remarks in mind, this chapter is organized as follows. First, we present an overview of how secondary education it structured and defined in SSA. We then provide a cursory survey of policy statements on secondary education in selected SSA countries. Finally, we look at central education ministry structures in selected SSA countries to consider strong and weak points, and at how decentralized offices are organized, how roles and responsibilities are assigned, and what challenges exist.

Structures and Functions of Lower and Upper Secondary Education in SSA

In order to understand how secondary education is governed in SSA countries, it is important to understand the general structures and function of secondary education systems in the region and the most important challenges facing those structures and functions.

Box 3. Defining Secondary Education

According to a general definition, secondary education belongs to an amorphous zone that lies between basic education and higher education. Secondary education is a step for pupils between the ages of 11 or 12 and 18. At this level, pupils are expected to broaden their knowledge and experiences from the basic level and prepare for work or higher education.

Source: UNESCO (2006).

Secondary education in SSA can be either academic, vocational or a mix of the two. General or academic secondary education is the *highway* to tertiary education (World Bank 2005) by contrast to vocational secondary education, which is considered a terminal degree that leads to the labor market (if there is one) but more often not closes the door on tertiary education.

Box 4. Vocational Training in Asia

"Traditionally, in many systems in Asia, vocational training is seen as an alternative route of education for those who are academically less able. The idea is to provide them with a skill that would keep (sic) them economically survive. This is increasingly difficult. First, there is no such skill . . . Second, most vocational training programmes are designed as a dead-end to learning."

Source: Cheng (2000), p. 52.

Almost every country in SSA divides secondary education into lower and upper programs of study, typically lasting between four and seven years. Lower secondary can last from two to four years (for students 11 to16 years of age) but most often lasts four years. Upper secondary usually lasts between two and four years for students aged 13 to 19 and most often lasts three years for students aged 16 to18. The divide between lower and upper corresponds more or less to a general education on the one hand and to specialized education on the other.

Lower secondary is most often a non-specialized continuation of primary education (UNESCO 2006) Where lower secondary vocational training does exist, it usually last three years for students aged 12 to 14 and is more often designed to provide students with "communication" and "life skills" rather than with skills for a market that increasingly requires more advanced academic skills (for example, accounting, market analysis, and literacy) (Holsinger and Cowell 2000). Upper secondary can prepare pupils for tertiary education or be the beginning of vocational training. SSA is not alone in struggling to define the dividing line between a general education and specialized training.

SSA countries divide lower and upper secondary differently, but some patterns are clear. Most francophone countries divide secondary education into two chunks of four and three years for lower and upper respectively.[6] The exceptions include the Democratic Republic of the Congo with a two-five split, Sao Tome/Principe with five years of lower and two years of upper secondary, and Guinea Bissau with three years of lower and two years of upper secondary and Rwanda with six years of secondary, the only francophone country without a lower-upper split. In Anglophone countries, the breakdown is more variable. The seven to eight years of secondary school are typically divided into two to four years of lower secondary and three to four years of upper secondary, with the exception of Kenya, which has four years of secondary education with no internal divisions.

Issues Facing the Structures and Functions of Secondary Education in SSA

SSA countries are facing a variety of challenges in their efforts to determine the appropriate structures and functions they need to have an effective secondary education system. The first issue they must face is that the academic skills needed to prepare pupils for higher education or for the labor market are rarely consolidated by the end of primary school. Remedial language and math training at the secondary level is an expensive and inefficient proposition, however, raising enter requirements when primary schools are ill-equipped to provide the quality of education needed to ensure basic literacy and math skills raises the issue of equity. Secondly, effective vocational training requires well-equipped facilities with the flexibility to align with changing labor markets and to offer low student-teacher ratios. Providing such facilities on anything but a limited basis is well beyond the means of most SSA governments. Third, SSA countries have scant experience on which to determine the appropriate mix of vocational and general education at the secondary level: at what point should vocational training begin? How integrated should it be with a more general secondary curriculum? Does general secondary education have a role beyond preparing students for tertiary education?

This report points to few if any differences in the management or accountability systems used in upper and lower secondary education. As a governance issue, however, determining the appropriate functions and structures of secondary schooling is among the most important decisions SSA countries will have to make in the coming decade. The purpose and objectives of upper and lower general and vocational secondary education need to be revisited, and provision of secondary education better aligned to serve these objectives. Such an examination may well have implications for the duration of basic as well as secondary education,

---

6. Angola, Benin, Botswana, Burkina Faso, Burundi, Cameroon, Central African Republic, Chad, Comoros, Congo, Cote d'Ivoire, Equatorial Guinea, Gabon, Guinea, Madagascar, Senegal, and Togo all have four-three splits.

and the pathways between general and vocational secondary education and between upper and lower secondary education.

SSA countries must eventually determine what constitutes free and universal education and therefore at what point a secondary education, to which access is limited begins and how access to that system is determined, They must also determine what structures best serve the purposes of a secondary system, and what represents the best divide between vocational education and preparation for tertiary education. Answering these questions may well challenge time-honored structures, or demand that those structures be used in different ways for different purposes. Whatever the answers in a given country, both academic and vocational secondary education must better prepare students for the workplace that they hope to enter.

Surveying the Policy Environment

Box 5. Secondary Education: A Policy Challenge

"Secondary education policy choices are . . . ambiguous and complex because of the intrinsic duality of secondary education . . . terminal and preparatory . . . general and vocational. The duality, complexity, and ambiguity of this level of schooling pose challenges for its provision. In the context of the soaring demand for secondary education, it is the responsibility of policymakers to . . . formulate secondary education policies designed to provide pathways and alternatives that will enable students to achieve their full potential."

Source: World Bank (2005), p. 15.

Most policy statements on secondary education in SSA make two claims: secondary education prepares citizens to lead productive lives and enhance national development; all citizens must possess certain social qualities to participate in a democratic process, and education can help instill these qualities. For example, the policy documents in Zambia, *Focus on Learning Strategies for Development of Education in Zambia* (1992) and *Educating our Future* (1996) declare that education serves individual, social and economic well-being and enhances the quality of life for all. They make academic and vocational training high priorities (Republic of Zambia 1996).

The South African government's Education White Paper of 1995 emphasizes quality for all and the redress of apartheid wrongs. The government's "vision is of a South Africa in which all our people have access to lifelong education and training opportunities, which will in turn contribute towards improving the quality of life and building a peaceful, prosperous and democratic society." The education mission is "To provide leadership in the construction of a South African education and training system for the 21st century" (Government of South Africa 2006).

In Senegal, the first education reform in 1971 sought to root education in local reality, ensuring that school programs, universities and staff were African. The National Education Law passed in 1991 led to a Ten-Year Program for Education and Training that focuses on universal primary education and also on technical training, with specific objectives for general and vocational secondary education.

It cannot be disputed that education is necessary for productive employment and that educated citizens are important for democracies. It is equally true that national economic well-being is intimately linked to an educated, employable populace. However true these statements are, few education policy statements define how much secondary education is necessary for employability or what kinds of and levels of knowledge and skills should be acquired in upper and lower secondary to make pupils employable and contribute to a productive economy. Few if any policy statements address the structure of lower and upper secondary and general and vocational secondary, their pathways and internal transitions. Furthermore they offer little rationale for the curriculum found within those pathways and divisions. Rare is the policy that clearly states specific objectives for secondary education. Finally, but certainly not least important, the issues of access and equity are rarely addressed carefully in policy statements. How many people should receive a secondary education? What is the basis of their selection, if secondary education is not universal? Does the number of people with a secondary education affect the democratic process? In general these are important issues which largely go unaddressed.

Some countries have, however, been able to move beyond generalizations and address very specific issues in their secondary education policy statements. In Senegal, the 1991 Ten-Year Education and Training Program, the most recent policy, makes the elimination of gender disparities in secondary education an explicit goal. It also seeks to lower the growth in numbers of general secondary students while strengthening the capacity of technical secondary and professional training (Republic of Senegal 2003). What it does not address is the contradiction between its desire to broadly strengthen technical and professional training and the fact that technical diplomas are highly specialized. In Kenya, the most recent Education Sector School Improvement Plan (KESSP) 2005–2010 explicitly addresses secondary education and sets targets and strategies for increasing secondary education transition/graduation rates (from 51 to 70 percent). The strategy focuses on increasing the numbers of and improving the quality of secondary day schools.[7] Both of these examples are good but partial starts on revisiting secondary education policies regarding access and linking education to the labor market.

It is understandable that few SSA governments have addressed secondary education in any depth. Their emphasis has been on universal primary education at least since Jomtien. However, as pressure rises for secondary education, SSA governments will need to develop more specific policies to direct secondary education and to define in greater detail the logic, structure, governance, management, and accountability of their secondary education systems. They will also address in greater detail the partnership with private providers of secondary education. The issues will require going beyond the regulation and licensing of private schools to ensuring greater accountability for the quality of the education in them. Addressing the most pressing secondary policy issues in SSA will demand:

- Specifying the purposes and objectives of secondary education. These specifications should define the structure, content, and duration of the program, the transitions between upper and lower and general and technical secondary education, and the pathways into and out of each track and segment.

---

7. Secondary day schools typically have poorer results than secondary boarding schools.

- Clarifying the relationship of secondary education and the labor market: to what degree and exactly how is schooling meant to prepare students for the world of work?
- Defining the roles and responsibilities of individuals at all levels and in all bodies governing education.
- Creating standards for student learning and an assessment mechanism to measure it.
- Revisiting access and selection mechanisms in light of equity issues.
- Refining the private-public partnerships to increase access, ensure the quality of education by private providers, and ensure accountability of private providers to the public.

These are just the first, but necessary, questions that SSA governments must address before they can successfully reform secondary education. Once the policy decisions are made, ministry structures and functions can be organized to accommodate them.

Box 6. Botswana: Successfully Planning for Expanded Secondary Education

Over a decade ago, Botswana became one of the first SSA countries to extend basic education to encompass junior secondary and to effectively focus on senior secondary education. Its flexible policy, rational planning and progressive adaptation of education management, teacher supply and curriculum offer an excellent example of for other SSA countries currently facing similar situations.

The process began in 1973. In response to rising enrollments in secondary education and an influx of inexperience teachers into Botswana, a Department of Secondary Education was created in the Ministry to assist, advise and guide teachers in preparing students for the Junior Certificate or Cambridge Overseas School Certificate Examinations. A specific centralized structure for secondary education was thus created. Four years later, at the first National Commission on Education, the government committed itself to universal access to nine years of schooling, making Botswana one of the first countries in SSA to extend basic education by encompassing junior secondary education. Senior secondary education enrollments were held to limits that reflected the need for human resources in higher education, further training and the labor market. The expansion of basic education inevitably increased demand for senior secondary education. By 1993, access to secondary education was growing as were professional concerns over the nature of the Cambridge Overseas School Certificate curriculum and its articulation with tertiary education. Botswana saw the need in the national economy for greater numbers of tertiary students, especially in the sciences, more enrollments at the College of Agriculture and the Polytechnic, and more teachers to accommodate the demand for more education. To address the issue and define an appropriate policy and implementation plan, a second National Commission on Education was organized. Its objectives are relevant to SSA countries today:

- Making education relevant to evolving national needs and objectives.
- Guarantee universal access to more solidly vocationalized basic education.
- Creating an education system that "responds to the aspirations of people and the manpower requirements of the country."

One of the strategies proposed was a unified five-year secondary school that merges junior and senior secondary education, without eliminating the single-level secondary schools, including junior secondary schools serving small communities.

Source: Botswana Ministry of Education, *Report of the National Commission on Education* (1993).

The Structure of SSA Ministries of Education

The division of responsibilities for education among government ministries varies across SSA countries. Some characteristics appear to be constant: (i) general and vocational secondary education are overseen by different divisions in central ministries; (ii) private education is overseen by a distinct division; and (iii) responsibility for managing teachers is often assigned to a teachers' service commission that enjoys semi-autonomy from the central ministry.

While secondary education is specifically named as a part of most central ministries, this is not true in Zambia (see Figure 1), where the ministry of education is organized by education function into offices that report to the Permanent Secretary. There is no clear designation of responsibility for any level of education.

Secondary education, from the organization chart, seems to be handled locally through the High School Boards, which report to the Provincial Education offices. The center of secondary school governance is thus three levels below the Permanent Secretary. The absence of horizontal lines of authority and responsibility among the different central education divisions and the absence of central ministry links with the decentralized local offices and secondary schools appears to fragment secondary governance. This fragmentation can cause extreme difficulty in managing secondary education. Examples of the management dilemma such fragmentation present include: How to concerns high School Boards raise with Provincial Offices reach the individuals procurement and supply offices who can resolve the issue? How can head teachers or school board assure that there concerns about teacher performance or professional development reach the Teacher Education Office and the Permanent Secretary? With no office in the ministry responsible for overseeing the secondary education system and with the possibility that information can be regarded as not significant enough to pass along it would be very difficult for a Permanent Secretary to get a full and complete picture, and very difficult, from the perspective of secondary school principals and teachers, to determine who has the authority to solve a problem and how to get through Provincial Offices to the central ministry to get something done.

In most cases, secondary education does figure in the ministerial structures, and most often lower and upper general secondary are housed together, while technical education is located in a different ministerial division.

We have seen that there is a trend towards lengthening basic education to consolidate learning during the early years. This can mean incorporating lower secondary into basic education. By extension, this could also mean offering vocational training in upper secondary, following the general trend in developed countries. If more SSA countries increase the number of years of primary education, they will also need to redesign the curriculum and pedagogical approaches. This raises a number of questions: Would expanded basic education be offered like primary education, with a single teacher per classroom? Or would extended primary education be structured like secondary school, with specialized teachers teaching different disciplines? Or would these additional years of primary education be a hybrid of primary and secondary school? Lengthening basic education also has consequences on the pathways to vocational secondary and to tertiary education. If basic education is longer, will vocational secondary begin only at upper secondary? If pupils acquire more general

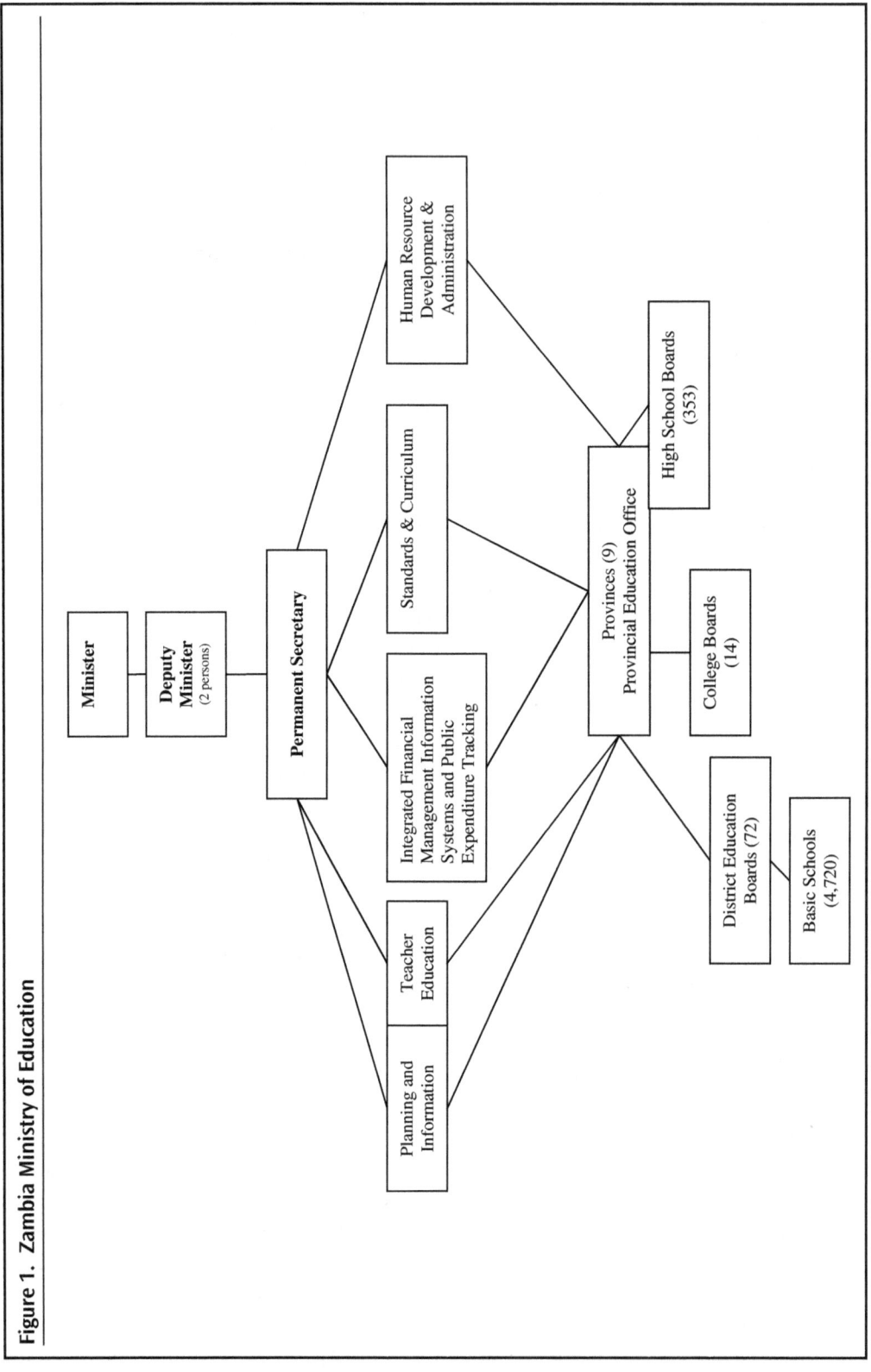

Figure 1. Zambia Ministry of Education

knowledge and competencies along with technical skills, would this open up a path between technical secondary and tertiary education? Policy decisions and legislation enacting the decisions need to address all of these issues.

Such decisions will not only affect the organization of central ministries, decentralized education offices, and schools, but also teacher training and deployment. Secondary school teachers and primary school teachers are trained differently, deployed differently, and paid differently. The lines of authority, responsibility, and communication between primary and secondary education divisions in a central ministry, its decentralized offices, and schools all have to be clear and designed to facilitate any required changes.

In the countries studied, responsibilities for general and technical secondary education are always assigned to different divisions in a central education ministry. At least a part of the differentiation is traditionally justified by the fact that secondary education may lead to university, but vocational education does not. For example, the Uganda Ministry of Education places these two forms of secondary education into a Department of Secondary Education, Business, and Technical and a Department of Vocational Education and Training (Uganda 2006). Secondary vocational students almost never continue to tertiary education. Francophone Senegal similarly separates the two educational tracks, but offers a highly stratified technical secondary education accompanied by specific diplomas, including very high level technical training that leads to technical institutes on a par with universities. This is a useful model if the training is well calibrated to the modern labor market and not a vestige of a moment in history when many different expert technicians were needed in an industrializing country.[8] But it also negates the justification for the separation of ministry divisions on the grounds that these forms of education prepare students for different future activities: students in both tracks can proceed to tertiary training.

It is not uncommon for ministries of education to fail to clarify the lines of authority and accountability between their functional divisions such as teacher training, curriculum design, and examinations, designated as semi-autonomous government agencies (SAGA), and sub-sector divisions such as primary, secondary and tertiary education. Examples include: What responsibility does the secondary education division have in regard to curriculum design? What if any responsibility does they have for assuring quality of teacher performance? One country in which such questions are pertinent is Kenya. The Ministry of Education, Science, and Technology (MOEST) is overseen by a Permanent Secretary, who is served by an Education Secretary, who oversees 10 divisions (including the sub-sectors of Pre-Primary Education, Basic Education, Technical and Vocational Education, Secondary and Higher Education, and Quality Assurance [teacher evaluation]) and several semi-autonomous institutions. The Kenya Teachers Service Commission (KTSC), which is responsible for teacher deployment, is one of these SAGAs, as is the Kenya Institute of Education (KIE), which is responsible for designing the curriculum. In addition to this complex set of relationships in the MOEST, the Ministry of Labour and Human Resource Development is "also involved in the provision of education, especially in technical education through the Youth Polytechnics and through industrial training programmes. . . . Public pre-employment training

---

8. The French education model in the 19th century became highly specialized, particularly under the various Napoleons who wanted to create a large cadre of highly trained scientists and technicians to ensure French economic superiority.

is also provided by specialized institutions under various other ministries and parastatals, for example the Ministries of Health and Agriculture, and Vocational Education and Apprenticeship" (Republic of Kenya 2006).

A governance structure with multiple lines of authority can obscure responsibility and authority and create managerial and accountability problems for schools. When, for example, inspectors in Kenya make recommendations to KIE about how well teachers are teaching, or when head teachers want to discipline teachers, the fact that teacher deployment is regulated by the KTSC subverts the authority of the head teacher and therefore his or her ability to hold teachers accountable. A governance structure must define clear lines of responsibility and channels of communication between divisions with overlapping and interdependent activities so that problems requiring action can be quickly resolved. In order to assure that reform objectives are met, a clear governance structure and consequent alignment and organization of divisions in central ministries are essential. Conditions for effective governance structures in the central ministry include:

- Educational policies that lead to clearly defined governance structures for all offices and institutions responsible of secondary education.
- Organizational structure for secondary education that are clearly aligned to serve educational objectives in the MoE and in its decentralized offices.
- Clear lines of authority and communication between divisions responsible for primary, secondary and tertiary education that ensure the effective and efficient transitions of learners between the sub-sectors.

Well defined lines of horizontal authority, which specify clear communication channels between and among the responsibility divisions.

Decentralized Education Offices

All SSA governments have decentralized responsibilities for secondary education to a greater or lesser degree. In most case, however, decisions making responsibilities remain highly centralized in SSA governments, reflecting cultural and administrative traditions. A complex architecture of the network of decentralized offices often means that schools send information through two or three levels before it reaches the central ministry. For such a network to work effectively, roles and responsibilities, processes and procedures must be defined and then implemented in an effective manner if policymakers are to know what is going on in upper and lower secondary schools and if that information is to guide policy.

Botswana's regional secondary education office provides an excellent example of well-defined responsibilities for a wide range of functions (Botswana Ministry of Education 2006; see Figure 2).

The process of decentralization is shifting more education management functions to regional offices, while keeping policy and planning at the central ministry. Obstacles to this becoming a more effective approach to governance, beyond the tradition of highly centralized authority, include the size of a country; the number of available trained, competent

Figure 2. Botswana Ministry of Education, Department of Secondary Education, Regional Structure

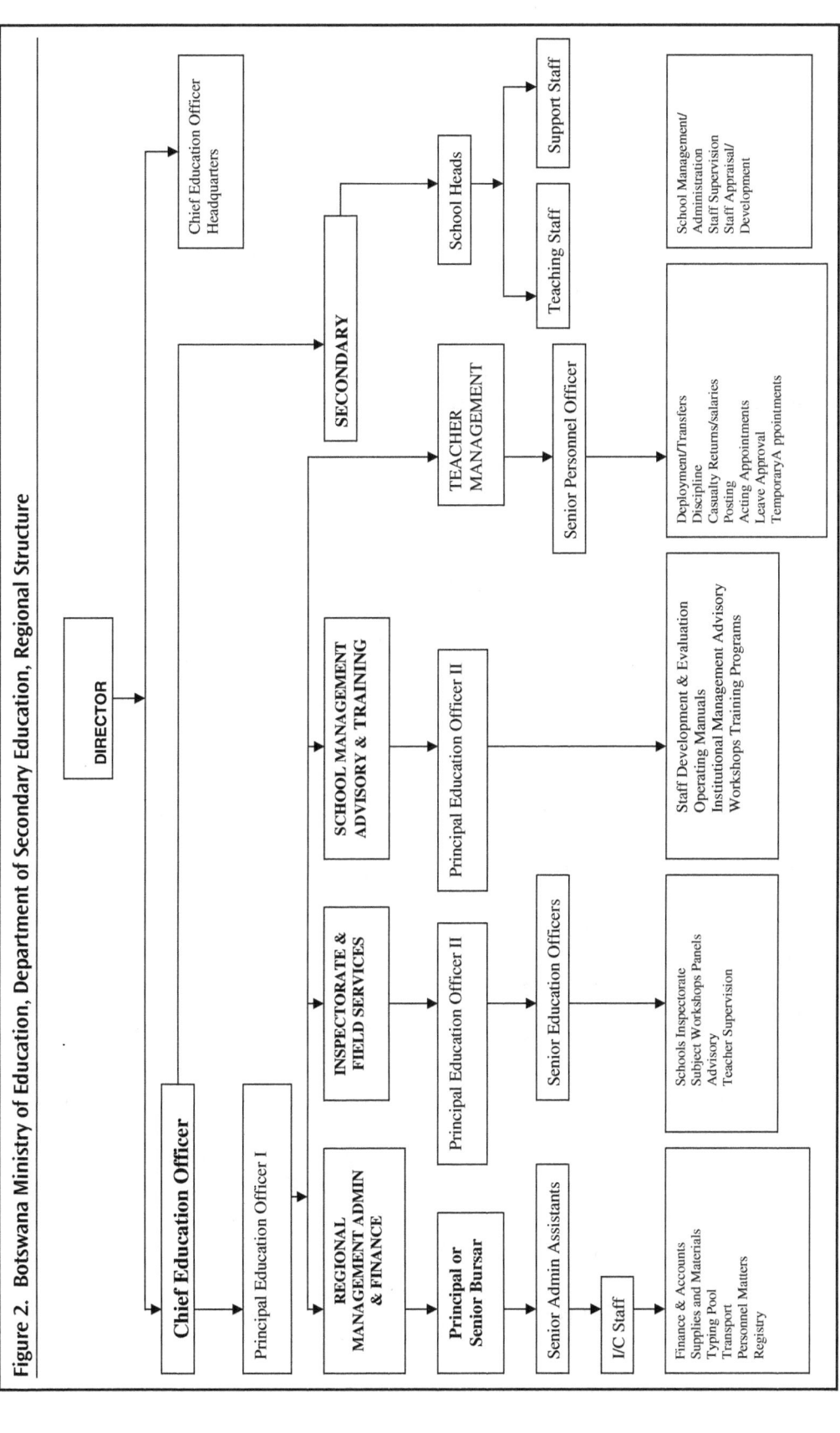

staff at the provinces or district levels, communications networks, infrastructure, and the prevailing culture of administration. A number of critical issues will need to be addressed for decentralization to make the governance of SSA's secondary education systems more effective.

First, for decentralized processes to be effective all personnel must be informed of and trained to carry out their roles in ways that are appropriate to their level of authority and responsibility. Chengo (2004) discussed the importance of this. In Zambia, the Ministry of Education decentralized and devolved power, authority and functions from national and provincial headquarters to the district, colleges and (high) school levels. Nine Provincial Education Offices monitor primary and secondary schools and oversee 72 District Education Boards, which are responsible for primary schools. There is little evidence, however that newly-appointed district education boards understand their roles and responsibilities or that they have capacity to fulfill them. Furthermore, the mandates and even the legal status of these entities remain to be defined. By contrast, in Kenya, the process of informing all offices of their roles and responsibilities has been quite successful. Evidence of this is obvious in the lowest or most local education offices. Municipal education officers are conversant with the government's most recent policy statements and can readily explain their own responsibilities and those of other education offices.

Second, to be effective, decentralized offices must be given the authority and the resources to do their assigned jobs. For example, in many countries, regional inspectorates are responsible for evaluating teachers. Each inspector is assigned a number of schools to visit and a schedule for visiting them. However, schools are often at great distances from the inspectorate office and from one another, and inspectors often lack the vehicles or gas to make the trips. No matter how well informed or trained they might be to do their jobs, they cannot do their work unless they have the resources. Resources include manpower: the number of trained staff in an inspectorate should be commensurate with the number of schools and teachers to evaluate. In Senegal, for example, education administration has been decentralized to the 11 regions or *académies* that offer different types of support services for secondary education. When secondary school principals request mentors for their teachers in a specific grade and for a particular discipline, a trainer is supposed to come on a temporary or prolonged basis to work in the school.[9] This flexible approach to teacher support is well designed, but the resources are not always available for inspectors in very high-demand disciplines.

Third, effective decentralization requires clear lines of communication from ministries to, from, and among decentralized offices. In South Africa, provincial and district offices seem to have some overlapping functions with respect to implementing policy. Provincial Offices have considerable latitude in structuring their offices. Some have devolved most decisionmaking to the district, while others have increased personnel at the circuit level (a district subset) to create multifunctional teams to work in schools; still others have set up large district offices covering many schools and large distances. District offices essentially monitor and support school activities. Keeping

---

9. The principal of Maurice Gueye Middle School indicated that the inspectors/teacher trainers function for two subjects (English and math) but work less well in the other disciplines. His schools were visited twice during the year by English and math teachers because they live in the area and actively organized extra seminars for teachers.

track of the activities of this variety of entities and ensuring that each office has the information it needs is a major undertaking.

Fourth, staff must be selected on the basis of their competence and be trained to carry out new responsibilities before taking them on. In Kenya, school Boards of Governors report to District Education Offices, which are the most local level of the education ministry. Board members are political appointees who do not necessarily possess either the skills or the interest to manage secondary schools nor is training a requirement for them.

Fifth, information must be regularly collected, analyzed, transmitted, and used as a basis for planning. There are many types of information that must be gathered and shared for an education system to function well. One example is information about primary school pupils moving to secondary schools. How many children will graduate? How many will enter secondary school? Are there special needs that secondary schools should accommodate? All of this information needs to be gathered from the primary school and transmitted through the education office so that a secondary school can ensure smooth transition. If the information is gathered, it must be analyzed; once analyzed, it must be transmitted in a timely way so that decisions can be made.

An example from Kenya suggests how poorly-aligned governance structures can thwart effective planning. Primary schools report to District Education Offices, and secondary schools are overseen by Provincial Education Offices. This means that the files of students who graduate from primary school are sent by that school to its District Education Office, which must in turn send the files to the Provincial Education Office. This latter office then sends the files to the appropriate secondary school.

> The transition from primary to secondary school is weakly structured, and pupil files are often lost. One of the biggest weaknesses is documentation. Reporting capacity needs to be improved by having the ministry define the necessary information, communicate and train at all levels. Ask a head of a primary school "who sat the exam;" he can't give you disaggregated graduation rates, gender information; there is a lack of capacity to analyze data.
>
> —Ali Atrash, Kenya School Improvement Project
> Mombasa, Kenya, September 2005

The example suggests that the process of gathering, analyzing, and transmitting information between education offices requires specific processes and skills, and clear channels for communicating. The need for such processes is particularly critical when responsibility for education sub-sectors is assigned to different ministerial divisions and decentralized offices.

Conclusion

These issues are summarized in the following table below. What must be borne in mind is the need for policy to guide objectives, for governance structures to serve the objectives, and for legislation to regulate activities so that a decentralized system can function effectively.

Box 7. Conclusions for Governance in the Education Ministry

Issues	Education Ministry	Decentralized Education Offices
The duration and objectives for general and technical secondary education must be clearly defined.	Ministerial responsibilities for the different types and levels of secondary education must be clearly assigned and aligned within the ministry in the manner that best serves educational objectives.	Legislation or regulation for decentralization must specify roles and responsibilities in decentralized education offices for different types and levels of secondary schools, including private schools.
The structures of, access to and transitions between upper and lower and general and technical secondary education must be aligned with education objectives.	The legislation governing the structure of, access to and the transition mechanisms for the different levels and types of secondary education must clearly define responsibilities throughout the education system.	Decentralized education offices must be regulated and organized to ensure effective mechanisms for access to and transition between the different levels and types of secondary schools, both public and private. Decentralized offices must have the resources and authority to implement effectively.
Decisionmaking and Lines of Authority	The regulatory framework for secondary education must designate lines of authority, roles and responsibility with all SAGAs (Teacher Training Commissions, Curriculum Design Divisions, Testing Divisions, Assessment Divisions, etc.) responsible for activities that cover all levels of education. Authority, roles and responsibilities must be clear, and include processes and procedures for communication and decisionmaking.	Decentralized education offices must have clearly delegated lines of authority and communication with central ministries, and with SAGAs.
Decisionmaking and Lines of Authority	Within the ministry and in its decentralized offices, the roles and responsibilities in primary, secondary and tertiary education must ensure the effective access to and transition between sub-sectors.	Decentralized education offices must have clearly regulated authority regarding primary, secondary and tertiary education, and processes for ensuring effective access to and transitions between sub-sector schools.

CHAPTER 4

Management of Secondary Education

Focus on the School

Governance structures extend from ministries of education through decentralized education offices to secondary schools, the point of confluence of governance structures and the public. In the previous chapter on governance, we discussed the visions for secondary education, the structures and functions of secondary education and the organization of central and decentralized ministries of education that steer education provision. In this chapter we discuss local education structure and function by way of addressing the management of secondary education. Of course, local education structures are a part of the governance structure, but we focus on schools under *management* to emphasize the importance of local management processes and procedures for the delivery of quality education.

Management procedures and processes include the rollout, in practice, of job roles and responsibilities, the gathering and transmission of information through different parts of the governance system, and decisionmaking. Strong management processes are also a precondition for accountability, which involves, among other things, making data transparent and available. In focusing on the structures that converge on a secondary school, the procedures involved in school management, and the responsibilities of a school head who does the managing, this chapter also touches on accountability issues; these issues are more fully presented in Chapter 5.

School Governance Structures and their Management

Secondary schools come under the purview of one or several central ministry and regional offices. In addition to these offices, all SSA governments have created and regulated local governance structures, which generally fall into two categories: (i) government-appointed high school governing boards or high school education boards, and (ii) participatory structures comprising, in the main, members of the local community. The latter most often consist of school management committees (SMCs) and parent-teacher associations (PTAs). For each of these groups, membership size, responsibilities of members, and the nature of the activities are all regulated. There are, however, occasionally overlapping functions and constituencies. There are also, on occasion, insufficiently articulated relationships between these groups.

One way to visualize the convergence of these groups is to take the example of Kenya. Each secondary school in Kenya is responsible to a district education office (DEO), a board of governors (BOG), and a parent-teacher association (PTA). The DEO, the most local ministry office, is a conduit of information from each school on enrollments, staffing needs, material needs, school conditions and academic information to the Provincial Director's Office (PDO) which then transmits it to the central ministry. BOGs were created by the Kenyan Education Act (KEA) in 1966 to establish a more direct link between the central ministry and secondary schools. BOG responsibilities were defined as overseeing school management in general and financial management in particular.

BOGs set secondary school fees using government guidelines, and ensure sound financial management, the mobilization of resources, the setting of priorities for spending and see that all expenditures are authorized. In addition, they oversee school facilities and monitor school performance. BOG members are appointed by the central ministry.

Each secondary school also has a PTA. PTAs were created after BOGs, by a Presidential Directive in 1980 and consequently have little real authority because they were a not created by the same legislation that created BOGs. PTA members are volunteers who through various means attempt to assess the quality of education offered in the school and express their opinions about that education. They also support the school's program by raising funds to supplement secondary school budgets and making decisions about the expenditures of these funds. An elected PTA executive committee is designated to liaise with the BOG. In practice, however, there is little liaison because the two bodies are generally in conflict. The PTA chairman can consult the BOG chairman who is required to present PTA concerns to the BOG, but in practice this reporting does not function well. PTAs usually voice their concerns at the BOG Annual General Meeting.

The school head is recognized by the government as an accountable officer. He is directly accountable to the DEO and to the BOG, and he is also supposed to report to the PTA (especially on the use of its resources). Unfortunately, PTAs complain that they have not been provided with the necessary documentation by the school head or by BOGs to be able to monitor finances and even understand how money is spent.

When a PTA, dissatisfied with the school head's financial management, voices its concerns to an unresponsive BOG chairman, it can go around the BOG and approach the relevant educational authorities. However, lacking access to documentation undercuts its ability to hold the school head accountable. For academic matters, the situation is mitigated because information about student academic progress, curricular activities, or general school results is more readily available. Nonetheless, holding the head teacher accountable is very difficult.[10]

In Zambia, the government has created and regulated High School Education Boards (HSEB) linking upper and lower secondary schools with ministry offices and the local civil

---

10. Ali Atrash, of the Kenya School Improvement Project, was an invaluable source of information for this description of secondary school governance bodies.

administration. HSEB members represent the district education office, the local administration, the school, and the PTA, and meet on an as-needed basis to oversee financial and general school management. Zambia's PTAs are elected, rather than voluntary, and raise funds for school materials and activities and also for teacher salaries. Thus, they feel somewhat responsible for teacher performance, a role that overlaps and occasionally puts them in conflict with the Zambian Teaching Service, which is responsible for hiring, deploying and firing teachers.

In Senegal, the recently created School Management Councils (SMC) for upper and lower secondary schools oversee the material and 'moral' activities of secondary schools, which span academic, administrative, and financial matters. They also ensure that the school complies with health regulations and responds to all questions from the Ministry of Education and the Education Inspectorate. SMC members are secondary school administrators and representatives from the Regional Council, the Mayor's Office, the local Treasury, the PTA and the student body. Parent-student associations (*association parent-élève*) exist in Senegal, but, according to some school heads, they are reticent about being involved.[11]

In South Africa, the 1996 Schools Act gave decisionmaking power to School Management Teams (SMTs) defined as internal management groups that include the principal, deputy head (where there is one) and department heads. These groups are responsible for daily and annual management and decisionmaking. The Schools Act also created School Governing Bodies (SGBs) that include the principal and elected representatives of parents, teachers, nonteaching staff and pupils. In South Africa, as in Zambia and Kenya, conflicts arise between governance bodies. Money is often the source of friction, as South African parents fund approximately half of all expenditures in most government-aided schools (Bennell and Sayed 2002) and they battle with SBGs and SMTs over school management. Financial support also creates friction between the churches and other religious and social groups (known as foundation bodies) that contribute funds and other support to the majority of government-aided schools in South Africa and the Ministry of Education. Foundation bodies have no formal responsibilities for governance and management, but their financial contribution gives them some claims on schools. School management is therefore complex for school heads because multiple sources of finance create multiple senses of ownership.

The problems of managing a complicated governance structure appear to be very similar in different SSA countries. Some suggestions for addressing these can be fairly straightforward. First, it helps immensely to have clearly defined lines of authority, responsibilities and reporting requirements among all parts of the structure. The simple existence of a governance structure does not guarantee that it will operate effectively. Second, clearly designated avenues to carry public voice to decisionmaking authorities are critical, along with guidelines for the responsiveness of government and local school management to the public. In Kenya, PTAs must rely on BOGs to transmit their messages up the ministerial ladder, but BOGs are politically appointed and may not feel compelled to take up the PTAs call or may gloss over a problematic situation when they pass it up the line. Third, secondary schools would benefit if governing board members were selected on the basis of their competence and their commitment to secondary education rather than solely for political reasons. The ideal configuration would be board members competent to manage secondary schools who also

---

11. Falou Dieng, Principal, Maurice Gueye Middle School, Senegal.

have good political connections. School governance and management stand to gain from changing some of these situations. If we imagine a PTA with greater ability to make its voice heard, its members may well be encouraged to participate with renewed energy.

School Leadership

> Much research has demonstrated that the quality of education depends primarily on the way schools are managed, more than on the abundance of available resources, and that the capacity of schools to improve teaching and learning is strongly influenced by the quality of the leadership provided by the head teacher. (IIEP 2000)

The emphasis on school leadership may be less pronounced in SSA than it is elsewhere in the world, but some studies are already pointing to the importance of school leadership for educational quality in SSA. One study suggests that SSA school leaders will become the focus of efforts to improve educational quality: "concerted effort to improve school leadership is one of the most promising points of intervention to raise the quality and efficiency of secondary education across Sub-Saharan Africa" (Mulkeen 2005). Further on, the study reports,

> recent literature on school reform suggests that principals or head teachers play a critical role in the success of strategies to improve teaching and learning. The knowledge they have of good teaching and learning practices, the leadership they provide for the school and community, and the ongoing support they give to teachers are all elements important to implementing successful school reforms.

Some SSA governments are already looking to school heads to improve educational quality. In South Africa, leadership training for secondary school heads has been designed in recognition of its importance, given the need to improve education quality. Senegal's School Improvement Plans (SIP), created in 1996, encourage the entrepreneurial skills of head teachers to find funding for school projects that enhance educational quality.

> School Plans provide an interesting opportunity for schools which are, in the main, entirely without funds. My school, for example, was awarded 4,188,000 CFA (approximately $8000) for such things as IT and internet, which encourage students to read, and improving the teaching of science, among other things.
>
> —Mr. Falou Dieng, Principal, Maurice Gueye Middle School, Senegal

If SSA governments are beginning to recognize the importance of school leadership, they may well revisit the selection criteria for school heads, the leadership training they receive, and how they are evaluated in their jobs. The following discussion addresses these issues, and concludes with some recommendations about ways to improve school management.

Who Heads Secondary Schools?

Virtually all secondary school heads in SSA are experienced teachers selected on the basis of their seniority: ". . . the process by which principals are selected is not based on qualifications to administer and manage a school, but rather they are selected based on prior positions held or their performances as teachers" (Mulkeen 2005). Seniority is one criterion for selection, but it may not be a sufficient quality for a job that is becoming increasingly complex. Some governments are realizing that even excellent, experienced teachers need training to be good head teachers. In Senegal, the government recognized that seniority was not necessarily the best criterion for selecting a secondary school head and even managed to persuade the powerful teachers' unions that a change needed to be made.[12]

How are Secondary School Heads Prepared for their Management Roles?

Secondary school heads receive some leadership training but rarely before starting their jobs. Nor does the training cover all the aspects of secondary school management that a head teacher will have to face; rather it usually focuses on the rules for reporting to the government. No teacher training institutes or universities offer advanced training or degrees in school leadership and management to prepare promising candidates to lead a secondary school. "Most principals do not have degrees in educational leadership. Rather, once they become principals, they may participate in in-service or distance education workshops to develop skills in needed areas. These workshops tend to focus on administration and management (*e.g.*, accountability, resource management, and record keeping)" (Mulkeen 2005). School heads themselves recognize that they need more and different kinds of training: "Areas in which principals need further training include information technology for financial management and evaluation, strategic planning, and human resource management" (Mulkeen 2005).

Training has an impact on how a school head perceives his/her role, and on how much of an impact s/he can have on the school. The government of South Africa has been concerned to align school management with classroom results and has emphasized instructional leadership. It has created a category for school principals and designated department heads as instructional leaders, making them responsible for integrating daily management, policy implementation, and curriculum delivery to get the desired learning outcomes. The South African Department of Education (DoE) has also established a requirement that all school principals be trained in leadership and school management, and has accredited courses for this purpose. The curriculum has been delivered largely by universities and NGOs to leaders already in their positions. In Senegal, the government created a specific training course on academic and administrative leadership for school heads, who were being asked to take over more and more types of school management. The course was delivered as in-service training from the provincial teacher support offices (Gershberg and Winkler 2003). Similarly, in Kenya, secondary school heads need to be trained, for currently, they "lack the analytical skills "[13] to know how to interpret the data that they collect and transmit to the District Education Offices.

What Does a Secondary School Head Do?

> You are the inspector, the financial manager, the curriculum implementer and the supervisor of teachers.
>
> —Khadija A. Said, Director, Sharif Nassir Girls' Secondary school,
> Mombasa, Kenya, September 2005

---

12. Mr. Falou Dieng, Principal, Maurice Gueye Middle School, Senegal.
13. Atrash Ali, Kenya School Improvement Project, Mombasa, Kenya, September, 2005.

Secondary school heads manage at least three different aspects of school life: academics, finances, and general administration. Academic management encompasses managing teachers and student learning. Financial management covers the management of the different funding streams received from the government, from student fees, and from extra-curricular activities organized by a school or a PTA. Administration covers the reporting to the local governance bodies—the decentralized education offices, school governing boards, PTAs, and internal management committees.

Academic Management

Academic management may be the most familiar task to head teachers, but managing teachers is complicated in SSA for many reasons, including the relative scarcity of teachers in some countries, poor pay, difficult working conditions, and a complicated governance structure for managing teachers. Indeed, while secondary school heads are called managers, their ability to exercise line management functions over teachers are quite limited by the governance structure.

Secondary schools have special issues, as they need highly trained teachers from specialized disciplines. Math and science teachers, in particular, are usually in high demand but less available than literature teachers, for example. Secondary school heads also have difficulties in managing teachers because the divisions that: i) oversee their hiring, deployment and firing; ii) evaluate them; and iii) are responsible for secondary education are themselves distinct. The lines of authority and responsibility—often unclear—complicate the relationships among entities. Kenya offers an example of how the centralization of teacher employment and deployment undercuts school management of teachers.

Responsibility for hiring, firing and deploying teachers in Kenya falls to the Kenya Teachers Service Commission (KTSC), a semi-autonomous government agency (SAGA). Its semi-autonomy comes from its position in the MOEST organization chart where it sits parallel to the division for Secondary and Higher Education which reports to the Education Secretary, and reports directly to the E Permanent Secretary. Deploying secondary school teachers follows a specific process. Secondary schools send monthly statistics to the Provincial Director of Education (PDE), indicating the losses in teaching staff due to death, retirement or natural attrition, by discipline. The PDE analyzes the data, and then requests teachers in the specified disciplines from the KTSC in Nairobi; no KTSC staff sit in local education offices. The high degree of centralization lengthens the process, but so does the shortage of teachers created by a previous freeze on teacher employment. Because only stopgap measures are being taken to replace departing staff, school heads are often simply unable to secure replacements.

Within Kenya, teacher evaluation comes under the aegis of the Quality Assurance (QA) division, one of the main divisions of the MOEST which, like the Division for Secondary and Higher Education, reports to the Education Secretary. A representative of the QA division sits in each District Education Office. The QA is responsible for school inspectors who monitor teaching quality. Inspectors' reports are submitted to the District's QA representative, routed to the Office of the Provincial Director of Education, where they are compiled and analyzed, and then sent to the MOEST QA division in Nairobi. From there, the connection with the division for higher and secondary education and with the KTSC requires several steps.

A realistic scenario helps illustrate the impact of this complex system for managing teachers in a secondary school. An inspector visits a school and finds that a teacher is doing a poor job. The inspector's report is submitted to the QA unit in the District Education Office, which transmits it to the Provincial Director's Office, which transmits it in turn to the QA division at MOEST. Someone from the QA division must meet with representatives from the Division for Higher and Secondary Education and from the KTSC. While all of this is taking place, the teacher continues to teach poorly and the head teacher can do little to change the behavior. To take another example, if a science teacher drops out during a term or if the secondary school has too many pupils and too few teachers, the school head requests teachers of the District Education Office, which routes the request to the Provincial Director's Office and onward to the KTSC. The school head has no direct link with KTSC or any way to create incentives to attract or reward good teachers or to discipline poor teachers. The governance structure and managerial processes thus limit the effectiveness of school heads to manage their teachers. The situation can be further complicated by teachers' unions.

Other dimensions of academic management include the procurement of books and materials, the creation of student tutorials, making courses available to adults or out-of-school youth, and the creation of extra-curricular activities that may be academic in nature. Many of these activities depend on funding, and a school head can create fund-raising activities to meet some of these needs.

Most importantly, a secondary school head is essentially held responsible for student achievement. In SSA, student achievement is typically measured by end-of-year and end-of-cycle high-stakes examinations over which the school head has little control. The school head can create opportunities for students to better prepare themselves, however, by designing tutorials or incentives. If a school head had greater incentives to use to motivate teachers, he could significantly affect educational quality. However, incentives for teachers are few, particularly in a system where seniority determines promotions and salary increases. Ultimately, then, academic management involves many things over which school heads have little control. If SSA governments turn to secondary school heads to help improve educational quality, they must remove at least some of the limitations created by current governance structures and management processes and procedures on school heads.

Financial Management

Secondary school heads must manage their budgets, which come from several sources: central governments provide some funding based on enrollments; student fees constitute the bulk of operating budgets; PTAs may contribute to the school coffers; and extra-curricular activities can produce some small benefits.[14] Financial management includes raising the needed funds, prioritizing needs and budgeting the available funds, spending only the limited amount available, and reporting expenditures in detail. Few school heads have training in these areas. Given the demands on their time, appropriate training in convenient locations would prove very useful.

Financial management could be improved both by finding alternative sources of funding to meet school needs and by improving the use and reporting of existing funds. One approach

---

14. Mr. Falou Dieng, Principal, Maurice Gueye Middle School, Senegal created a competitive cyber café in his school.

that seems to address both areas for improvement is the initiative to generate School Improvement Plans (SIPs) in Senegal. SIPs were created there in 1996 as competitions for funding school projects. A SIP specifies its goal or goals, links them to activities and a timetable and includes costs estimates justified by pro forma receipts (see the Senegal case study). The SIP is sent through a series of approvals at different levels to determine whether or not it is complete and viable, and ultimately forwarded to the Observation Group for School Improvement Plans and the MoE, which submits it in turn to donors. Once awarded, funds are sent to the regional inspectorate, which makes them available to the school SMC's bank account. All expenses must be justified and meet the terms of the SIP. Thus, in a single initiative, school heads find an additional source of funds and practice (and assistance) in strong financial management procedures.

Box 8. School Improvement Plans in Senegal

"School Improvement Plans (SIPs) provide an interesting opportunity for schools which are, in the main, entirely without funds. My school, for example, got an award this year for 4,188,000 CFA (approximately $8000) for such things as ICT and internet, encouraging reading, improving the teaching of science, etc."

Source: Mr. Falou Dieng, Principal, Maurice Gueye Middle School, Rufisque, Dakar.

Reporting

A secondary school head reports to several governance structures, each with its particular membership, mandate, and allegiances. The local education offices require vital education statistics: enrollments, student progress, numbers and disciplines of active teachers, condition of the physical plant, and finances. In Zambia, for example, secondary school heads submit quarterly reports on progress and finance to district offices who pass them on to provincial offices and finally to the central ministry. The provincial offices resolve those problems that they can and forward the reports to the MoE, which consolidates them to identify issues for immediate attention.

Secondary school heads also report to their boards of governors, which tend to focus on financial management. Boards of Governors (BOGs) often include political appointees and representatives from local administrations whose loyalty may or may not be primarily to the schools. A school head must be able to respond to queries and may have to work hard to ensure that the BOG has the interests of the school at heart. For example, a BOG can be more or less attentive to school funding from local and governmental sources and can affect the speed with which funds reach the school and how they are used. It can transmit demands from the secondary school head to the offices that might react to them with greater or less alacrity, or work with greater or less energy to make sure that school demands are heard. Energetic BOGs can even attend to the quality of the education offered in the school and can bring their competence to bear. Reporting to BOGs, therefore, could have very different effects on a school, depending in part on the school head's ability to analyze the issues and make the case for addressing them, and in part on the capabilities and motivation of members of the BOG.

Because PTAs are concerned with both the quality of education and the expenditure of funds, school heads must be able to appropriately display and discuss information on student and school performance and on finances, analyze the information in a helpful way, and propose positive actions. School heads can be more or less entrepreneurial and more or less engaged with their PTA. Training school heads in these skills could turn out to be very effective at improving education at secondary schools.

Effective reporting to education offices, a BOG, and a PTA requires that head teachers can assess school strengths, weaknesses, and needs in academic and financial areas and then prepare accurate and compelling written and oral documents to support their assessments. The value of training in understanding what information should be presented in what fashion could be palpable here. With more effective documentation, central ministries could act more quickly and responsibly. A secondary school head who appreciates the value of information and can analyze it and propose solutions to the issues it raises will be both a good advocate and a dynamic part of the governance structure. Well-trained, effective school leaders would even increase the chances that SSA governments could get outside support in improving educational quality.

Conclusion

The process of decentralization of education in SSA has raised growing expectations of secondary school heads. They are potential leaders for educational change and, in many countries, are expected to initiate or contribute to such change. The discussion in this chapter touched on the different governance structures that converge on secondary schools and on the roles of secondary school heads in managing the various elements of the structure. Well-designed and timed leadership training for talented secondary school leaders could benefit the national education system by equipping these leaders with the skills and encouragement to collect important information, analyze and display it, and argue for its use in improving the education offered at their schools.

Improved secondary education management systems at the local level will require:

- Clearly delineated and defined roles, responsibilities and authorities among different governance and management structures for specific objective and processes.
- The selection and training of all staff on the basis clearly identified competences.
- Delegation of the authority needed to carry out designated roles and responsibilities.
- Clearly defined channels of communication and decision taking.
- System of accountability that reward success and provide appropriate corrective action for failure.
- Timely and reliable information on which to base decisionmaking.

CHAPTER 5

Accountability

SSA governments are seeking ways to improve the quality of secondary education in their countries. As we saw in the preceding chapter, governments worldwide are turning to school leaders to improve educational quality and are responding to greater demands for accountability from the public for the education system where children are learning. This chapter focuses on ways in which SSA governments can make their education systems accountable to the requirements set by the government, to the students they serve, and to parents and the community in which the school is located. We use a series of terms to describe different kinds of accountability: *upward accountability* refers to the obligation within the school hierarchy to report to those above school management; *downward accountability* to an obligation that the school hierarchy has to learners, and *outward accountability* to the responsibility that the school system has to community members (and especially those who pay school fees).[15] Accountability pertains *to* all education providers *for* the education service that they provide *to* the public.

This chapter begins by discussing the two major sources of information that governments have on how well the education system is working. The first source is the reporting through government channels (upward accountability); the second source is the evaluation of student learning (downward accountability), which may come from student participation in high-stakes end-of-year examinations or ongoing assessment or national assessment. In the final section, we discuss the reporting of information outward, to parents and to the community.

---

15. South Africa's Minister of Education, Asmar Kamal, discussing his efforts to improve accountability in South Africa.

Upward Accountability

Earlier chapters have outlined many sorts of reporting that can satisfy the requirements of upward accountability. Specifically, school heads may present required data to their local ministry offices, governing bodies, and PTAs; and well-defined lines of communication ensure that the data make their way up to the central ministry offices, down to students, and out to the community. In addition, most education ministries have an inspectorate that employs experienced educators to visit and evaluate teachers. These evaluations can supplement the information provided by school heads and, when used well, enhance the quality of education offered by the school. In Uganda, the Education Standards Agency, created to support an overwhelmed inspectorate, has evaluated secondary schools. In South Africa, the ministry has introduced a practice of whole-school evaluation that challenges the notion of a teacher inspectorate, suggesting rather a process of checking all aspects of the education offered by a school. The following sections therefore discuss inspectorates in general and then the South Africa and Uganda experiences in particular.

Inspectorates and Accountability

In each of the countries examined for this study, school inspectors regularly visit teachers in a set of schools, observing their classes, and preparing a report for the ministry on what they have seen. The idea is both that teachers will know they are subject to evaluation and potentially to sanctions, if they are not performing well, and the ministry's staff responsible for teachers will find out where there are problems and be able to move to correct them. Increasingly, however, the inspectors are being asked to take on the role of *mentor* for teachers, as they can provide in-service support along with their evaluations.

In Senegal, for example, in addition to the usual inspectors charged with visiting a set of schools, the ministry employs inspectors with a specialty in a specific discipline or grade to serve as mentors, providing in-service training for longer or shorter periods of time. Secondary school heads can request support for a teacher to work in the school; depending on availability and needs, teachers can rotate through several schools needing teachers support in a given discipline or remain in one school for a period of time. The ministry has even created the position of inspector for heads of schools, which is particularly useful because few heads receive sufficient training before they begin their jobs.

Unfortunately, the implementation of such a system has met with difficulties. Inspectors are not always available for the disciplines requested; they may lack the vehicles needed to get to the school; or they may simply not be able to stay in a school as long as they are needed. This approach to organizing an inspectorate to provide in-service training, has the potential of bringing needed information to teachers in a timely manner and of following up initial training efforts. It requires significant resources and management to ensure that it delivers on its promises.

In order for an inspectorate to improve teacher performance, the inspectors need a smooth and effective way of transmitting their findings upward within the ministry. Clear roles and responsibilities within the ministry must then ensure that staff can act on the information they receive, solve problems, and act. However, as we saw in the earlier chapter on governance, many ministries have multiple groups dealing with information on teachers, such as Kenya's Quality Assurance Division and its independent

Teachers Service Commission. Good accountability requires that these various groups work together to analyze the inspectors' reports and act appropriately to improve teacher performance.

South Africa's Whole-School Evaluation (WSE)

South Africa has recently implemented a National Policy on Whole-School Evaluation (WSE), adapted from a policy of the British Office for Standards in Education. WSE is

> a monitoring and evaluation model that is radically different from the previous school inspections carried out in South Africa under the apartheid regime. Together with the accompanying guidelines, this Policy prescribes an approach that is built upon interactive and transparent processes . . . include[ing] school self-evaluation, ongoing district-based support, monitoring and development and external evaluations conducted by the supervisory units. (Asmal 2000)

The WSE thus uses internal or self-evaluations and external or outside evaluations to look at an individual school. Its processes and tools are built on nationally agreed-upon criteria and methodology, so all schools are held to the same requirements. After all parts of the evaluation have been completed, participants discuss the results and the schools put improvement plans in place. The government employs trained individuals to help schools set reasonable, attainable targets for change. Provincial and national decisionmakers receive the results for each school, so they can use them as a basis on which to improve the country's practices and education policy.

Whole-school evaluation has considerable potential as an accountability mechanism in that it brings local stakeholders together for an in-depth evaluation of a school, looks at a wide variety of facets of education (not simply teachers), uses instruments based on national standards to facilitate comparisons with other schools, and informs both local and national education planning. In reality, it has faced problems. Politically, it met with opposition from teachers' unions fearful that many educators would be unable to handle the range of questions and meet the evaluation standards. Materially, WSE staff lacked sufficient trained personnel and vehicles to reach all schools in a reasonable time frame.

Uganda's Secondary School Evaluation

Created in 2001 to help an overwhelmed Inspectorate Department to evaluate secondary schools, Uganda's Education Standards Agency (ESA) had a broad mandate that included the development of systematic approaches to inspection and evaluation of all levels of schools and the improvement of the quality of education practices. Like South Africa, this evaluation was slated to look broadly at secondary schools. Using expert comments and advice to generate recommendations, ESA's 2003 report suggested that public secondary schools needed more monitoring and accountability. Specifically, it indicated that: (i) Boards of Governors needed to be trained and monitored; (ii) schools needed to comply with the financial regulations; and (iii) that teacher management was wanting (Education Standards Agency 2003). The Ministry rejected the findings; head teachers and other school administrators resented the evaluation and extended their resentment to the Education Standards Agency (Bennell and Sayed 2002).

This example demonstrates many of the difficulties of introducing a new accountability mechanism. A new education agency must have a clear role and set of responsibilities, acknowledged by all levels of the education structure. The introduction of a new form of school examination must be carefully managed to mitigate the kind of conflict that was generated by the Education Standards Agency's evaluation.

Downward Accountability

This second type of accountability has considerable importance to an education system: it is the accountability of the system for student learning, an accountability that ensures that the business of education is producing the desired end product. The fact of the matter is that much of the reporting required within education systems, whether it is upward, downward, or outward, concerns the *inputs* to education—policies, legislation, regulations, the organization of education offices, the curriculum, teacher training, teaching materials, finances, the status of school facilities, and so forth. All of these inputs are important to the ability of an education system to function. They need to be attended to in order for students to learn. However, the success of an education system should be measured, as well, by its *outputs*, which are educated children. In this section of the chapter, we discuss how governments can be held accountable for student learning, beginning with their setting of standards for that learning.

Setting Learning Standards

The basis of a system for measuring student learning is a body of standards that specifies just what a student should know at the end of each stage of learning. Standards should incorporate knowledge, skills, and competencies in each subject matter of the curriculum. Generally, such standards are set by the government in discussion and negotiation with educators from universities and secondary schools. They may be judged against international databases of educational standards to ensure that a graduate in an SSA country who meets that country's standards compares favorably with a graduate in other countries. In addition to the standards, then, ministries must put in place systems for designing, administering, scoring, and reporting on the assessments to evaluate just what students have learned.

In the countries that this study surveyed, secondary education policies rarely establish either standards or the mechanisms for evaluating pupils' learning achievements at given levels. Rather, students take very high-stakes examinations that determine whether or not they move on to the next cycle of education—from primary to lower secondary, from lower to upper secondary, and from upper secondary to tertiary. These examinations may or may not assess the breadth of knowledge, the variety of skills, and the underlying competencies that educators believe a graduate should have; they have not been judged by such criteria. Their purpose is to give schools at the next level of education a benchmark for selecting students, not for finding out whether they shave acquired the substantive knowledge that they need to succeed.

Assessments of Student Learning

Once a country has established standards for learning, it is also important to assess whether students meet those standards. There is a range of accountability models from which to choose in doing such an assessment, and the design of data gathering must meet the country's needs for information. Options include:

- An end-of-year or end-of-cycle examination (such as those usually used in SSA) that tests every student in every content area and results in a decision of whether or not the child is promoted. This is viewed as a "high stakes" examination because passing has such a significant effect on a child's life.
- An end-of-year or end-of-cycle examination that tests every student in every content area and results in a judgment of a school or a district. The No Child Left Behind program in the United States falls into this category. State-designed examinations are given to every child in specified content areas, and the results are used to judge the effectiveness of a school and a district. Sanctions apply to individual schools, districts, and states in which an insufficient number of students pass.
- A periodic national assessment of learning for children of a particular age or grade to provide an aggregate picture of student knowledge. The National Assessment of Educational Progress in the United States is an example of such an examination. A national discussion in conferences and the press provides feedback to educators on the degree to which students are meeting national expectations. International tests such as TIMSS also fall into this category. Such examinations might also correlate other information (for example, attendance, socio-economic status, and disability status) with level of student learning.
- An examination embedded in a larger research project, such as an assessment of student learning along with an assessment of teacher capability and behavior. This kind of project can contribute to our knowledge base on such topics as best practices in teacher training.

South Africa is unique among the SSA countries studied, in that it has grade-level standards in its Revised National Curriculum Statements and has assessed student performance at grades 3, 6, and 9 to assess the degree to which students met the standards. However, teachers and teachers' unions reacted against this idea of evaluating schools through the measurement of student learning. They raised concerns that the study's focus on learner performance was not a good proxy for a valid examination of the education system. The education system within this country, and presumably many others in SSA, is comfortable with evaluating students in a high stakes situation, but not yet in using the results to evaluate the performance of schools.

While few African countries have participated in major international studies and only South Africa participated in TIMSS, the utility of national assessments is well recognized by many SSA Ministers of Education. For example, 47 African countries participated in the Monitoring Learning Achievement (MLA) project. MLA I assessed grade 4 pupils in literacy, numeracy and life skills; and MLA II tested grade 8 pupils in mathematics and science. MLA included questions about student background, school characteristics, and family background (Kelleghan and Greaney 2004).

> **Box 9. South Africa's Experience with International Assessments**
>
> "South Africa's experience with TIMSS and TIMSS-R underlines the problems facing implementers of international assessments. Howie (1999) noted that deadlines imposed by organizers can be difficult, if not impossible, to meet in situations where there may be no mail or telephone services or funds for travel to schools. Other problems include lack of accurate population data on schools; poor management skills; insufficient attention to detail, especially in editing, coding, and data capture; lack of funding to support project workers; and difficulty in securing quality printing on time. Instructions to test administrators, for example to walk up and down the aisle, are obviously inappropriate when classrooms do not have an aisle."
>
> *Source:* Kellagan and Greany (1996), p. 45.

Twelve francophone countries grouped together in the PASEC[16] and 15 Anglophone countries grouped in SACMEQ[17] have joined to examine their national education systems and to build capacity in them to carry out cooperative education policy research. They believe such an evaluation will "promote capacity building by equipping educational planners in member countries with the technical skills needed to effectively monitor and evaluate schooling and the quality of education. In providing valid and accessible information systems as a basis for decisionmaking, [they also seek] to promote stakeholder involvement and greater transparency." To date, the assessments have only been carried out for primary education (Kellaghan and Greaney 2004).

Designing a national assessment requires very specific skills (Kellaghan and Greaney 1996) and can have unforeseen consequences,[18] particularly when the assessment reports results in "a way that would appear to permit international comparisons" (Kellaghan & Greaney 1996). The potential for uncomfortable comparisons, however, should not dissuade governments from carrying out assessments that provide data on which they could base important decisions.

In their discussion of the effects of national assessments in SSA on education policy, on teaching, on the curriculum, and on schools, Kellaghan and Greaney found that assessments were rarely used to inform policymakers about their education systems. When senior education personnel in Ethiopia, Malawi, Niger, Nigeria, South Africa and Uganda were interviewed,

> Respondents reported that while the findings of national assessments sometimes were covered in the media, in none of the six countries did they feature in parliamentary debate.

---

16. *Programme d'analyse des systèmes éducatifs des Pays de la CONFEMEN des ministres de l'éducation des pays ayant le français en partage,* the Education Systems Analysis group of francophone Ministers of Education: Burkina Faso, Cameroon, the Central African Republic, the Republic of Congo, Cote d'Ivoire, Djibouti, Guinea, Madagascar, Mali, Niger, Senegal, and Togo.

17. Southern and Eastern African Consortium for Monitoring Educational Quality. SACMEC has completed two major cross-national studies of education quality. SACMEQ I (1995–1999) was completed by seven Ministries of Education (Kenya, Malawi, Mauritius, Namibia, Tanzania (Zanzibar), Zambia, and Zimbabwe). The SACMEQ II Project (2000–2003) was completed by fourteen Ministries of Education.

18. The OECD and Statistics Canada collaborated on a study of literacy in about 1995 that initially included nine countries. The results of the study indicated that France was number eight after Poland. Before the publication went to press, the French government withdrew because of the possible repercussions for the education minister. Another country had already withdrawn from the study for similar reasons.

In only one country were the findings used to justify the granting of additional resources to schools. In four countries, the results were shared with curriculum authorities, but in only two countries was feedback provided to teachers or schools, and in only one country was feedback provided to textbook publishers. Respondents in Ethiopia and Nigeria said that the national assessment results had not been used in the formulation of educational policy. (Mulkeen 2005)

Assessments of student learning provide a picture of how well students are learning. The picture should be analyzed at high levels to translate performance into actions to resolve problems. These actions can touch upon every aspect of the education system, and include things such as changing a math curriculum, improving teacher training, providing more or different textbooks for a particular discipline, or lengthening the school year or hours of daily contact. The picture provided by a student assessment should also be transparent: the public should be told the state of its education system in a way that encourages its understanding and provides channels for making its voice heard. The entire process of assessing student learning and responding to the results is a far more thorough accountability mechanism than end-of-cycle high stakes examinations or an evaluation of teachers carried out by teaching inspectorates.

Outward Accountability

> Schools aren't accountable to the community . . . to make schools more accountable to the public, make head teachers' job descriptions include informing the public of results. This is assumed now and needs to be specified . . .
> There is little consultation locally. More local accountability would improve education.
>
> —Kenya Interviews

Outward accountability, or reporting to the public, requires that transparent, meaningful information about the education system be accessible and comprehensible to those outside of the education system. In addition, it means that a recognized mechanism exists for the public to express its opinions, otherwise known as *voice*.

We have already seen that most SSA governments have created participatory education structures (school management committees and PTAs) to encourage the involvement of parents and the community in education. "Involv[ing] parents and community members in school governance as per governance standards . . . is perhaps the most common form of accountability reform supported by donors." This involvement of parents and community members in school governance is the most common form of accountability, and should include a clear indication of the standards that schools are to meet. For parents to hold school accountable, they must know the standards to which schools are to be held. The existence, availability and comprehensibility of information are the *sine qua non* of these accountability mechanisms. Information has to be provided in an appropriate format to be easily understood, and training must be provided if it is needed to ensure that the public understands the information.

Participatory structures, we have also noted, must also provide avenues for parents to voice their opinions. To recall the discussion of the relationship between PTAs and Boards of Governors (BOGs) in Kenya, we saw that there is no officially determined and recognized link between these two structures. The absence of a structure to link the two bodies means that parents have no officially sanctioned channel through which to voice their concerns to the BOG, which is a conduit to higher levels of the education ministry. Where the government does not define and establish channels of communication that ultimately make it responsive to parents, communities, or civil society in general, outward accountability does not exist.

Outward accountability can be assured when:

- Transparent data (on student performance, financial management, school management) is accessible to the public.
- Standards against which to judge performance are defined and shared.
- Stakeholders receive the support needed to ensure that they have the capacity to analyze information.
- Defined, recognized mechanisms are established to transmit public voice to authorities that can respond.
- Authorities are responsive to public opinions.

Thus far, outward accountability has been used as a general term for notifying the public of all educational inputs and results. One specific area of interest to the community is school finances. As we saw in the previous chapter on management, secondary school heads are fiscally responsible for monies coming from the government, the PTA and parents (through school fees). And all contributors have a stake in ensuring that their monies are spent well. In Kenya, for example, the MOEST has sought to make secondary schools more accountable by depositing funds directly into a school bank account and asking for reports on expenditures. Accounting to the different funding groups has been successful, according to the Director for Higher and Secondary Education,[19] because schools have been given responsibility and authority for funds and communities know it and demand accountability, just as the government has done.

This is one sort of step towards making schools accountable for their funding. Other mechanisms are posting budgets on school walls, reporting on budget expenditures at PTA meetings, and presenting written comparisons of budgets and expenditures to High School Boards of Governors.

School grading systems or "School Report Cards" are another example of an innovative accountability practice that has been used in South Africa. Community members grade a school on a number of things, including teacher performance, children's attendance and school achievement. The grades are posted on the school wall. When visitors come to the school, they fill out a register indicating what they have seen and would like to see during the next visit. This widens the level of accountability to the school cluster and education office personnel responsible for the school, by making public the shortcomings and the demands for improved performance.

In Parana State in Brazil, school report cards provide parents and communities with information on student achievements measured against reasonable expectations. In Chile, a national system measures student performance, and a system for teacher incentives provides school-level group incentives based partly on student performance and partly on

---

19. Mr. David Siele, Director of Secondary and Higher Education, Ministry of Education and Sports, Nairobi, Kenya.

community satisfaction. Chile provides all citizens, including politicians, with information on school performance in grades 4, 8, and 10 every third year and on municipal averages. School results are provided to parents and made available generally. Results for individual schools are compared to all schools and to schools in similar socioeconomic conditions (SIMCE 2006). Chile has created innovative systems for teacher and school rewards based explicitly on nationally measured student performance (World Bank 2006). In addition, it has designed a framework for quality teaching and individual teacher awards and sanctions and used it as a basis for teacher evaluations (Docente Mas 2006).

Conclusion

Accountability mechanisms in the education system in SSA are in their infancy. Many ministries have reporting relationships (a) between schools and district or provincial offices and then (b) among ministry offices that could constitute upward accountability, but information does not always pass expeditiously from its source to its end point. In general, the information that is asked for concerns the inputs needed for a good education: facilities, materials, teachers, etc. Few ministries have embraced the concept of downward accountability, or the notion that they are accountable for the output of a good education (student learning). Most SSA countries do not have learning standards for the various grades and subjects against which to judge student achievement or a mechanism for assessing it. Finally, outward accountability of the school system to parents and the community is also only beginning. Some PTAs learn details about how their monies are spent; many do not. It is a rare school or country that gives itself a thorough report card—and is fully accountable.

To achieve accountability secondary school system will need to assure that:

- Secondary education policy clearly states educational objectives and standards and establishes a mechanism for measuring whether students meet those standards.
- National assessment systems are designed to measure student learning.
- Education systems have clearly defined reporting relationships, so that all levels of the education hierarchy know what data should be sent to what parties on what timetable.
- The roles of inspectors are clearly defined, they are provided with the resources to carry out their duties, and their findings are a significant part of evaluating teacher performance.
- There are effective upward and downward decisionmaking and information-sharing processes.
- Defined, recognized channels exist for the public to be informed about education issues, the progress of students, the policies under consideration, and the expenditure of funds.
- Parents and community members receive the support they need to ensure that they can analyze the financial and academic information.
- Channels exist to allow the public to have its voice heard and regulations and procedures are in place to ensure government responsiveness to public voice.
- Rewards and sanctions exist and are implemented for the performance of systems and individuals.

CHAPTER 6

The Governance and Accountability of Private Schools

There are a number of special issues that SSA countries must address in assuring that their secondary education systems meet the needs of their citizenry and support their emerging economies. This section will explore two of these—the role of private schools and the provision of ICT.

Private Secondary Education in Sub-Saharan Africa

This chapter focuses on private secondary schools, which are proliferating in SSA. As we have seen in previous chapters, ministries are struggling to set and enforce policy concerning private schools with which they collaborate in a *de facto* private-public partnership to provide secondary education. In most countries, private schools must go through a process of registration before they can open, suggesting that the ministry of education has basic requirements for a school that it can enforce. In many countries, the ministry of education supplies teachers for private schools, which suggests it should have a role in monitoring teacher performance. If a country were to have standards of learning, the ministry would presumably be responsible for ensuring that private schools met such standards like government-funded schools. Yet, enforcing any regulation in private schools is problematic for many SSA governments. On the one hand, ministries do not have sufficient trained staff to monitor and enforce rules in government schools, let alone in the private sector. On the other hand, the private school funders and owners are not particularly interested in government intervention in what they consider their affair. With both sides of the public-private partnership shying away from government intervention, it is not surprising that such intervention is minimal.

The current situation calls for government attention because private schools will continue to proliferate in response to market demand. All secondary schools in SSA are fee-based, whether they are private or public. However, there are not sufficient slots in public secondary schools in SSA to meet student demand. As a result, there are considerable numbers of private secondary schools. For example, of the 5,500 secondary schools in South Africa, more than 1,557 (28 percent) are independent. In Senegal, there are nearly equal numbers of private and public upper and lower secondary schools, and the number of private schools is growing rapidly. In Dakar, the country's capital, the number of private lower secondary schools rose from 88 to 111 (26 percent) between 1997 and 2003, compared to the increase in public schools from 49 to 52 (6 percent) during the same period. Private technical schools have also proliferated in Senegal. Though they are expensive to construct, outfit and run, well-supplied technical schools can be profitable, particularly when they offer significantly better facilities than a public school.

With the proliferation of private secondary schools, it should be a part of the role of government to hold the private sector accountable to the public for the quality of its service. The government, after all, works in partnership with the private sector in many endeavors. It sets regulations for the public good and should enforce them. The central question of the chapter, then, is: what mechanisms work to allow governments to effectively manage private schools?

Regulatory Mechanisms

The creation and operation of private secondary schools are regulated by SSA governments. All the countries in this study require private schools to obtain licenses before they open. In Kenya, for example, the government has clear procedures for opening a community secondary school (see Box 10). Before beginning operation, the community or private school owners must petition the district education office for instructions. The government responds by sending an inspector to verify the facilities and to see whether a government or British system curriculum is going to be used. A written inspection report is sent to the ministry as part of the registration process, and a regulatory agency ensures that the paperwork is in place before issuing the license.

The problems with the registration process are largely ones of manpower. The group trying to start a school may experience considerable delay in getting inspectors to visit; forms get lost as they make their way through the ministerial hierarchy; the committee that needs to review each application may not meet for several weeks; letters of authorization may take a very long time to arrive. Clear procedures notwithstanding, few governments are able to be responsive. A private school may open in anticipation of being registered, and government monitoring is sufficiently slack that no one may stop its operation.

Assuming that parents have any options when choosing a private secondary school, the following accountability mechanisms could both ensure that regulations are met and give parents data as a basis for make their choice:

- If a government imposes financial and other sanctions when there is evidence that a private school does not meet regulations.

> **Box 10. Procedure for Opening a Private School in Kenya**
>
> - Application for registration of a school is made in a prescribed form and is submitted to the Registrar through the District/Municipal/City Education Officer.
> - Application form is accompanied by the following documents:
>   — Inspection report from the Public Health Officer indicating whether the institution complies with the set of health standards.
>   — Inspection report from the inspector of schools of the given district where the school is located.
>   — Minutes of the District Education Board (DEB) in which the application was discussed.
>   — Certification of registration of business name from the Registrar General.
>   — An application for the approval of the district manager.
>   — Names of school managers and copies of their academic and professional certificates.
>   — School size in terms of land (rules differ depending on locality).
>   — Proof of ownership of the land on which the proposed school is or is to be built.
> - Once the Registrar receives the application, it is presented to the Ministerial Committee on Registration of schools for evaluation in accordance with the relevant provisions.
> - If the application is approved, it is forwarded to the Ministry of Education for necessary authorization.
> - The Minister then issue (sic) two letters to the manager of the school approving and authorizing the operation of the school.
> - The Registrar of the school will then issue a certificate to the institution after the final inspection.
>
> *Source:* Onsomu and others (2004).

- When information is readily available to the public about the licensing process for private schools, their funding, and the veracity of their claims in general.
  - In Kenya, the rankings of the country's top 100 schools, judged on the basis of end-of-cycle examinations, are published in the newspaper. Not only are school results advertised nationally, but parents are also informed about their children's results which they can compare with national rankings.
  - The Association for the Development of Education in Africa has created an education journalism award, precisely to promote greater public information and interest in education. Encouraging education journalism would be a useful step to increasing accountability in private schools, if sufficient comparative information (on success rates on examinations, on fees, on facilities) can be obtained. Articles praising schools that do a good job could be powerful incentives for other schools to open their doors to the press.
- Creating and enforcing policies that assure that private schools have stakeholder based governance structures similar to for private schools. could increase accountability.
  - In Kenya, management boards oversee private secondary schools and provide information to the government.
  - In Argentina the Confederation of Private Education Institutions (*La Confederación Argentina de Instituciones Educativas Privadas* Website 2006).

- The Independent Schools Association of Southern Africa (ISASA) offer accreditation which involves having member schools meet management and educational criteria and subscribe to a code of ethics.

To assure productive public-private partnerships in secondary education and to improve governance, management and accountability of private secondary schools, SSA countries should:

- Establish legislation for private schools that defines requirements for licensing and standards for a quality education.
- Assure that government support personnel are available to monitor private schools and ensure they are meeting the required standards.
- Require that information which allows parents and teachers to make informed judgments about private school performance are readily available.
- Create governance bodies and participatory structures (for example, boards of governors or parent-teacher associations) for private secondary schools like those in public schools.

CHAPTER 7

Special Issue

Addressing ICT and Technical Training

Because of the importance of ICT in the global economy and because of the spread of computer applications as a tool for communicating, the question in Africa education is not whether computing skills need to be taught, but how soon it will be affordable and practicable to teach such skills in secondary schools and in what way ICT skills should be introduced. . . . Botswana may be the only country in Sub-Saharan Africa that has embarked upon system-wide implementation of computer education in public secondary schools. . . . African countries can learn by staying informed about the Botswana experience (e.g., how to cope with cost, maintenance, and staffing constraints).

—Lauglo (2004)

The use of ICT in secondary schools can be considered an index both of the modernization of secondary education in general and vocational education in particular, and also an index of the degree of adaptation to the global economy. A recent study of the use of ICT in 36 schools in Benin, Cameroon, Ghana, Mali and Senegal, the largest study ever conducted on ICT and education in West and Central Africa, involved over 66,000 students and 3,000 primary and secondary school teachers, school heads, and parents.[20] The process of introducing ICT and the current status of ICT varies by country. In Cameroon, a presidential initiative to introduce ICT into all secondary schools has not yet led to a clear policy. In Benin, entrepreneurial initiatives to use ICT to train drop-outs and government initiatives both rely on outside contractors. In Ghana, parents contribute to many ICT initiatives. In Mali, computers were installed in schools without any human resources training to accompany them.

> For the sake of scientific and technological development, I would argue for a rethinking of secondary technical education that is responsive to the technological development of Ghana. . . . The rapid development of Ghana, and Africa, in the twenty-first century would

---

20. ERNWACA and the University of Montreal, draft transnational study of ICT in African education.

depend more on an increasing provision and support of secondary technical education of a higher quality that is geared to a technologically-oriented, world-informed and dynamic. (Quist 2003)

In Senegal, a national ICT policy is in its initial phases. The education ministries use ICT for communication and data storage, but there has not been sufficient coordination across units. In October 2000 the MoE began a study to produce an ICT planning tool and to improve the coordination across various education sectors in the Ministry for Technical and Vocational Training, the Ministry for the Elimination of Illiteracy and the Promotion of National Languages, and the Ministry for the Family and Early Childhood. However, study results have yet to be fully implemented. The Ten-Year Education and Training Policy Document considers that ICT is necessary for improving the quality of education and for modernizing the education system, but the implementation of this has required outside funding. The World Links project was introduced in 1997 and funded by the World Bank as a means of increasing access to online lessons for secondary students and teachers. Many urban high schools and a few middle schools have been outfitted with computer equipment and many teachers have been trained. That is, 500 computers have been delivered, and 500 teachers and approximately 20,000 pupils have received training in data processing and teaching applications. While regional efforts have been made to outfit secondary schools with ICT equipment, in the main, there has been no centrally funded effort to oversee the implementation of the policy goals.

The use of ICT in secondary schools is costly, requires a number of conditions that are not easily satisfied in SSA countries (for example, stable supply of electricity, training for teachers, and ongoing maintenance of machines). What is necessary for the effective use of ICT, and what is required to make this possible at what levels of education are problems that SSA educational system are not likely to solve with significant levels of private-public partnerships.

CHAPTER 8

Recommendations

This matrix of the central governance, management, and accountability issues facing secondary schools in SSA is designed to serve as a roadmap to those addressing the overarching issues who must be mindful of the consequences for governance, management and accountability.

National Level

Issues	Governance Recommendations	Management Recommendations	Accountability Recommendations
Structure of the Secondary Education System	The duration, objectives, access and transition mechanisms for all levels and types of private and public secondary education must be established by legislation and a clear regulatory framework. The organization and provision of secondary education must respond to contemporary needs and realities. **Example:** International trends indicate a rising demand for skills and competences. PISA evaluates applied learning among 15 year-olds of math, science, and language learning.	Ministries of Education must define process and procedures for managing all types of secondary education and for collaborating effectively with SAGAs (teacher training, curriculum design, examination division, etc.). Management for secondary education must involve clear lines of responsibility and collaboration with primary and tertiary divisions to maximize the effectiveness of transition.	The structures for secondary education must clearly address issues related to how free, universal education is defined and at what point, through what processes individuals are given access to higher levels of education.
Roles and Responsibilities of Ministries of Education	Within central Ministries of Education, authority for secondary education must be clearly designated. Clear lines of authority as well as the roles and responsibilities of the SAGAs that affect secondary education (Teachers Service Commissions, Curriculum Service, etc.) must also be defined in ways that promote effective oversight for secondary education. This will require a systemic perspective on education.	Ministries of Education need clear line of authority and decisionmaking between various levels, divisions and structure involved in managing the secondary education system.	Ministries of Education must ensure effective governance and management of secondary education and assure that the information needed for effective decisionmaking is available to the government and to the public.

Local Steering Mechanisms for Secondary School	The legislation concerning school governance bodies must clearly delineate authority and roles and responsibilities to avoid overlaps, gaps, or conflicts among them. Sufficient resources and training, where needed, must be allocated.	Secondary schools governance boards, including PTAs, SMCs, and BOGs, must be managed according to established procedures. Reports on activities must be made and transmitted to designated authorities on a regular basis.	There must be process and structures to assure that local governance groups are responsible to their constituencies.
Head Teacher School Leadership	Leadership training should be integrated into teacher training in a timely manner, given heightened expectations of school leadership. Example: In South Africa, leadership training for secondary school heads has been designed in recognition of the need to improve education quality. Whole School Evaluations have been promoted to improve educational quality from the school level.	School leaders should be selected on the basis of proven competence. School leaders must have clear roles, responsibilities, and lines of reporting to all school governance bodies and education offices.	The performance of school leaders should be regularly monitored against established indicators and results communicated to education offices and to the public.
The Management and Use of Information	Education data management systems must be in place and have the resources to ensure the collection of timely and accurate education data at all levels of the education system. Example: Zambia's Basic Education Sub-Sector Programme 1999–2006 included an EMIS project to improve the capabilities of the Ministry of Education to collect, organize, process, store, share, and disseminate education information as a basis education planning and management at all levels. All levels of the education ministry and schools need to gather, analyze, and transmit education data regularly.	Clear processes and procedures for timely, accurate data management must be established system-wide, and clear lines of communication established between secondary education divisions and SAGAs. Education staff at all levels of the education system must be competent in the dimension of data management for which they are responsible.	Reliable, transparent data must be available to a wide range of decisionmaking. Decisionmakers have skills and capacities to effectively use date.

(continued)

National Level (*Continued*)

Issues	Governance Recommendations	Management Recommendations	Accountability Recommendations
Upward Accountability within the Education System	Governments should establish national educational norms and standards, and assessments of student learning to determine compliance. The necessary structures and mechanisms must be created to carry them out.	Ministries of Education must establish system-wide processes and procedures to design, administer, and analyze assessments and their results.	Ministries of Education must report regularly on education results to the government and be held accountable for them.
Downward Accountability to Students	National assessments should be established to inform governments about the quality of their education systems.	Staff at every level must be trained to implement assessments.	Education results must be made available to students on a regular basis.
Outward Accountability to Parents and Community	Ministries of Education should have clear frameworks for reporting education data internally and to the public. Clearly designated channels must be established for public voice. Clear channels and timetables must be established for government response.	All levels of the education system must be informed of and trained to report regularly on education data, and to comply with *ad hoc* demands for data.	Reliable, transparent education data, including financial data, must be made accessible to the public. The public must have clearly designated channels for voicing its concerns to parties able to respond to them.
Private Secondary Schools	The creation and operation of private secondary schools requires clear regulatory frameworks to ensure accountability. SSA governments can establish legislation linking financial support to private schools to their accountability.	Private secondary school providers must manage secondary schools in accordance with government regulations.	To be accountable for the quality of the education they provide, private schools should be encouraged to participate in national student assessments and publish the results of national examinations.
ICT	SSA governments need to examine the legislation and regulatory framework around ICT.	Every SSA government must develop a plan for managing the integration of ICT into education for management and learning.	

Decentralized Education Offices

Issues	Governance Recommendation	Management Recommendations	Accountability Recommendations
Structure of the Secondary Education System	Decentralized education offices need a regulatory framework defining authority, roles and responsibilities for providing and managing all levels and types of regional secondary schools. Clear communication protocols must be defined with the central ministry, with SAGAs, with other sub-sector offices, and with schools.	Decentralized education offices must clearly delineated responsibilities and clear protocols for reporting and decisionmaking.	System for regular communication, reporting and assessment of all aspects of regional secondary schools should be established and maintained.
Education Policy	Decentralization legislation or regulations must specify authority, funding, roles and responsibilities in decentralized education offices for secondary education.	All staff must be informed of and trained to carry out responsibilities. Clear definitions of responsibility, management processes and procedures for all activities must be established. Example: Botswana's regional secondary education offices have clearly defined staff roles and responsibilities.	Decentralized offices must report to education offices and to schools on the implementation of education policy in their areas of responsibility on a regular basis.
Local Steering Mechanisms for Secondary School	Legislation of steering mechanisms must designate responsibility for oversight and support from decentralized offices, including the timely transmission of data and resources.	Decentralized Education offices should facilitate the operation of local steering mechanisms by respecting legislation and providing management support.	Decentralized education offices should ensure timely reporting of local steering mechanisms and the transmission of reports and data to the central ministry for action, where needed, on a timely basis.

(continued)

Decentralized Education Offices (*Continued*)

Issues	Governance Recommendation	Management Recommendations	Accountability Recommendations
Head Teacher—School Leadership	Decentralized education offices must have the authority to provide school heads with necessary resources to carry out their responsibilities (education data, teachers, teacher support, training, etc.)	Decentralized education offices must have establishes protocols for managing all resources, including data, teacher support, training, or funding. Effective processes and procedures must be in place for linking school heads with central ministry divisions or SAGAs, if needed.	Decentralized education offices must be accountable to head teachers and schools for the services they provide. An accountability mechanism akin to the school report card could be created as a 'decentralized office' report card.
Information Management and Use	Decentralized education offices must have the resources and competent staff to manage data effectively. All dimensions of data collection (reporting mechanisms and calendars, aggregation, cleaning, analysis, transmission) must be specified and resources allocated for them to be carried out.	Clear processes and procedures should be in place regarding all pertinent aspects of data management. Staff should be selected on the basis of competence and trained on data management.	Transparent, reliable education data must be transmitted to ministries, schools and the public.
Upward Accountability Within the Education System	Decentralized education offices must have data collection and reporting protocols on all dimensions of secondary education. Mechanisms must be established and the necessary resources allocated to ensure the transmission of timely, relevant data.	Decentralized education offices must have procedures for managing education data, and competent trained staff who can report to education ministries regularly.	Decentralized education offices must provide high-quality data regularly to ministries and schools.

Downward Accountability to Students	Decentralized offices need a regulatory framework and the authority to ensure high quality regional education services. Channels must be created for students to voice their demands. Channels must be created to ensure responsiveness to student voice.	Decentralized education offices must have clear processes and capacity to provide quality secondary education services and data, as needed, for students.	Decentralized education offices must ensure high quality secondary education for students.
Outward Accountability to Parents and Community	Decentralized education offices must have the authority and resources to ensure high quality regional secondary education.	Decentralized education offices must provide high-quality education for the community, and provide transparent, reliable education data to schools, communities and parents	Decentralized education offices must report to the public regularly on regional secondary provision and quality.
Private Schools	Decentralized offices should have the authority and resources to oversee and monitor the creation and operation of all private regional schools. Example: Procedures for opening a private school are easily available in municipal offices in Kenya	Decentralized offices must have the resources and protocols to implement the regulations for creating and operating private schools.	Decentralized offices and private schools should provide the public with data on the quality of education provided in private schools. Regional media awareness raising campaigns organized by decentralized education offices could improve the public's grasp of quality and cost issues in private secondary schools.
ICT		Decentralized education offices should have the capacity to advise schools on the use of ICT as a management or learning tool in regional secondary schools	Data on comparative costs and benefits of ICT hardware of software should be made public and accessible as a basis for any decisionmaking.

Secondary School Level

Issues	Governance Recommendations	Management Recommendations	Accountability Recommendations
Structure of the Secondary Education System	The structure of secondary schools must be aligned with education objectives. The secondary education system—the provision of education and administrative services—requires a regulatory framework appropriate to national objectives, needs, and means.	Each secondary school must manage teachers, budgets, and reporting to local steering bodies effectively and have clear processes and procedures for linking them with education offices to do so.	
Education Policy	Legislation regarding the establishment and operation of school need to clear delineated in legislation.	Secondary schools must be managed in compliance with education policy.	
Roles and Responsibilities of Education Ministry	Ministries need clear guidelines and procedures of effectively decentralizing the education system.	School managers must be informed of their obligations to the education ministry.	Secondary schools must report regularly to all education offices and provide timely, reliable data.
Local Steering Mechanisms for Secondary School	The legislation and regulation of school governance bodies must clearly designate authority and define roles and responsibilities to avoid overlaps or gaps and conflicts.	Secondary schools governance boards members (PTAs, SMCs, BOGs) must be selected on the basis of competence, informed of and trained to carry out their responsibilities.	There should be mandated channels for assuring public voice and timetables for government response to stakeholder concerns.
Head Teacher— School Leadership	Leadership training should be integrated into teacher training in a timely manner, given heightened expectations of school leadership. **Example:** In South Africa, leadership training for secondary school heads has been designed in recognition of the need to improve education quality. Whole School Evaluations have been promoted to improve educational quality from the school level.	School leaders should be selected on the basis of proven competence. School leaders must have clear roles, responsibilities, and lines of reporting to all school governance bodies and education offices. All entrepreneurial activities need to be	The performance of school leaders should be monitored by the governance bodies and the community. School leaders should regularly report to their constituencies.

Information Management and Use	The regulation of data management and reporting must be clearly disseminated in all secondary schools.	Secondary school managers must have the competence and protocols for managing education data.
		Secondary schools must manage information data in compliance with regulations, and report to the ministry and to the public on their compliance.
Upward Accountability Within the Education System	Reporting responsibilities for school leaders must be clearly regulated and the resources allocated to ensure that all responsibilities can be met in a timely fashion.	Secondary schools must manage the collection and transmission of education and financial data effectively and in a timely manner.
		Secondary schools must provide timely, accurate education data to the education offices to which it reports.
Downward Accountability to Students	The decentralization of teacher management shows promise for addressing teacher deployment and support issues.	School managers should be responsible of the quality of teaching and learning in their schools.
		Secondary schools must make relevant education data accessible to students in a timely manner.
Outward Accountability to Parents and the Community	Regulations regarding responsibilities of school heads should include accountability to the public.	School heads must report regularly to PTAs and to individual parents on school operations.
		Secondary school heads must make education data and results accessible to parents and to the community in clearly designated ways.
Private Schools	The creation and operation of all types and levels of private secondary schools must be regulated and resources allocated to ensure that regulations are accessible and complied with. Example: Procedures for opening a private school are easily available in municipal offices in Kenya	Private secondary school funders and managers must comply with regulations and be accountable for the services they provide.
		Linking support with accountability measures can encourage school compliance. In South Africa, funding mechanisms are accompanied by a series of norms that provide accountability incentives for school directors.
		Public posting of school results.
ICT	Evaluations of the cost-benefits of the use of ICT for education should precede legislation. Private-public partnerships to provide ICT should be facilitated.	Entrepreneurial schools should be encouraged to fund well-defined ICT projects.
		Secondary schools must report on the costs and use of ICT to funders and to the public and assess the cost-benefit relationship.

APPENDIXES

APPENDIX A

Terms of Reference

1. How are roles and responsibilities distributed between the national ministries of education at regional, district, and school levels regarding both junior and senior education? How are accountability relationships established between the levels?
2. At public junior and senior secondary education levels, how are the different governing tools (legal, financial, establishing goals monitoring, pre- and in-service training) used, and are they used in alignment?
3. Is the current division of roles and responsibilities between the national level and the lower levels of management, including the public and private junior and senior secondary schools, conducive to efficient use of resources and the quality and relevance of teaching and learning? By agreement, this TOR has not been addressed.
4. How can public junior and senior secondary schools be made more accountable and to whom, for the quality of their organization and delivery of quality education to all students?
5. How can parents, local community, local industry and the students themselves be brought into such an accountability process?
6. What is the governance structure for private schools? What is the legal framework regulating their operation?
7. How can private junior and senior secondary schools be made more accountable, and to whom, for the quality of their organization and delivery of quality education to students?
8. How can assessment and evaluations methods be applied constructively for monitoring and improving quality in this context? What is the role of an inspectorate, (if any)?
9. How are teachers managed regarding utilization, deployment, monitoring and evaluation of their work, and what incentives/sanctions are applied in the management of teachers?

APPENDIX B

Years of Compulsory, Primary, Lower and Upper Secondary Education

Country	Compulsory	Primary	Lower	Upper	Total Secondary
Angola	8	4	4	3	7
Benin	6	6	4	3	7
Botswana	...	7	2	3	5
Burkina Faso	7	6	4	3	7
Burundi	6	6	4	3	7
Cameroon	6	6	4	3	7
Cape Verde	6	6	3	3	6
CAF	6	6	4	3	7
Chad	6	6	4	3	7
Comoros	9	6	4	3	7
Congo	10	6	4	3	7
Cote d'Ivoire	6	6	4	3	7
DRC	...	6	2	4	6
Eq. Guinea	5	5	4	3	7
Eritrea	7	5	2	4	6
Ethiopia	6	6	2	4	6
Gabon	10	6	4	3	7
Gambia	...	6	3	3	6

(continued)

Country	Compulsory	Primary	Lower	Upper	Total Secondary
Ghana	8	6	4	3	7
Guinea	6	6	4	3	7
Guinea Bissau	6	6	3	2	5
Kenya	8	8	4*	4	4
Lesotho	7	7	3	2	5
Liberia	10	6	3	3	6
Madagascar	6	5	4	3	7
Malawi	8	6	2	2	6
Mali	9	6 (9)	3	3	6
Mauritania	6	6	3	3	6
Mauritius	7	6	3	4	7
Mozambique	7	5	2	5	7
Namibia	10	7		5	5
Niger	8	6	4	3	7
Nigeria	6	6	3	3	6
Rwanda	6	7		6	6
Sao Tome/Principe	4	6	5	2	5
Senegal	6	6	4	3	7
Sierra Leone	...	6	5	2	6
Somalia	8	8	—	4	5
South Africa	9	7	3	2	5
Sudan	8	8	—	3	5
Swaziland	7	7	3	2	5
Togo	6	6	4	3	7
Uganda	...	7	4	2	6
Tanzania	7	7	4	2	6
Zambia	7	7	2	3	5
Zimbabwe	8	7	—	6	6

Source: UNESCO, *General Education Statistics 2005*; UNESCO *World Education Report 2000.*

APPENDIX C

Decentralization Matrix

Education/General	Administrative	Fiscal	Political
Deconcentration to Regional Government Offices and Regional MOE Offices	Move managerial decisions and managerial accountability to regional offices of central government and MOE.	Give regional managers greater authority to allocate and reallocate budgets.	Create regional, elected bodies to advise regional managers.
Devolution to regional or local governments	Education sector managers are appointed by elected officials at local or regional level.	Give sub-national governments power to allocate education spending and, in some cases, to determine spending levels (i.e., through raising revenues).	Elected regional or local officials of general purpose governments are ultimately accountable both to voters and to sources of finance for the delivery of schooling.
Delegation to schools and/or school councils	School principals and/or school councils empowered to make personnel, curriculum, and some spending decisions.	School principals and/or school councils receive government funding and can allocate spending and raise revenues locally.	School councils are elected or appointed, sometimes with power to name school principals.
Implicit delegation to community schools	School principals and/or community school councils make all decisions.	Self-financing with some government subsidies, especially in remote areas where public schools are not present.	School councils are often popularly elected.

Source: Gershberg and Winkler 2003.

Bibliography

Abdul-Hamid, H. 1995. *Assessment of Student Learning Outcomes in Southern and Eastern Africa: Lessons Learned from SACMEQ Study.* Washington, D.C.: The World Bank.

Acedo, C., ed. 2002. *Case Studies in Secondary Education Reform.* Improving Educational Quality Project, American Institutes for Research. Washington: USAID.

Ahmed, M. 2000. "Promoting Public-Private Partnership in Health and Education: The Case of Bangladesh." In *Public-Private Partnerships in the Social Sector: Issues and Country Experiences in Asia and the Pacific.* Manila: Asian Development Bank Institute

Arcelo, A. A. 2000. "Public-Private Partnership in the Philippine Education Sector." In *Public-Private Partnerships in the Social Sector: Issues and Country Experiences in Asia and the Pacific.* Manila: Asian Development Bank Institute

Asmal, Kader. 1999. *Call to Action: Mobilising Citizens to Build a South African Education and Training System for the 21st century.* Pretoria: Press Release.

———. 2000. "Opening Address." Proceedings of the Conference on The National Policy on Whole School Evaluation. Government Gazette Staatskoerant no. 215395. Cape Town.

———. 2002. "Opening Address to JET Education Services." Proceedings of the Conference: Balancing Support and Accountability to Improve School Performance. Johannesburg: JET.

Atchoarena, D. and P. Esquieu. 2002. *Private Technical and Vocational Education in Sub-Saharan Africa: Provision Patterns and Policy Issues.* Paris: IIEP.

Batoko, O. 2004. "Leadership for Reform and Modernization of Governance" Seminar on Public Sector Leadership Capacity Development for Good Governance in Africa. Kampala.

Bennell, P., G. Bulwani, and M. Musikanga. 2003. "Secondary Education in Zambia: A Situational Analysis with Special Reference to Cost and Funding Issues." Report

Commissioned by the World Bank Secondary Education in Africa (SEIA) Research Program. Centre for International Education, University of Sussex.

Bennell, P., and Y. Sayed. 2002. "Improving the Management and Internal Efficiency of Post-Primary Education and Training in Uganda." University of Sussex.

Bloom, D. E., P. Craig, and M. Mitchell. 2000. "Public and Private Roles in Providing and Financing Social Services: Health and Education." In *Public-Private Partnerships in the Social Sector: Issues and Country Experiences in Asia and the Pacific.* Manila: Asian Development Bank Institute.

Botswana Ministry of Education. 1993. *Report of the National Commission on Education.* Retrieved July 14, 2006 from www.moe.gov.bw/headquarters/rnpe.

———. 2006. "Republic of Botswana: Gaborone." Retrieved March 16, 2006 from http://www.moe.gov.bw/dse/index.html

Bregman, Jacob. 2004. "Trends in secondary education in OECD countries." Paper presented at Second Conference on secondary education in Africa. Dakar.

Bregman, J., and K. Bryner. 2003. *The Quality of Secondary Education in Africa.* Paris: Association for the Development of Education in Africa (ADEA). Draft monograph available at http://www.adeanet.org/biennial2003/papers/7A_Bregman_ENG.pdf

Briseid, Ole, and Francoise Caillods. 2004. *Trends in Secondary Education in Industrialized Countries: Are they relevant for African countries?* Policies and Strategies in Secondary Education. Paris: IIEP, UNESCO.

Calfee, Corinne, Drake R. Warrick, and G. Caldwell. 2003. *EMIS and Related Activities, First Quarter Progress Report.* Washington, D.C.: American Institutes for Research.

Cheng, K. 2000. "Information Era and Lifelong Learning: Public-Private Partnership in East Asian Culture." In *Public-Private Partnerships in the Social Sector: Issues and Country Experiences in Asia and the Pacific.* Manila: Asian Development Bank Institute.

Chengo, A. 2004. *High School Policy Issues and Current Practices in Zambia.* Lusaka: Zambia Ministry of Education.

Chinsamy, B. 2002. *Successful School Improvement and the Educational District in South Africa: Some Emerging Propositions.* Developed under the District Development Support Program Project. Washington, D.C.: USAID.

Coffey, E., and L. Lashway. 2001. "Trends and Issues: School Reform." *Abstracts, Clearinghouse on Educational Policy and Management.* Oregon: College of Education, University of Oregon. Retrieved July 15, 2006 from cepm.uoregon.edu/trends_issues

La Confederación Argentina de Instituciones Educativas Privadas. 2006. "La Confederación Argentina de Instituciones Educativas Privadas." Retrieved March 16, 2006 from http://www.caiep.com.ar/index.html

De Grauwe, A. and others. 2005. "Does Decentralization Lead to School Improvement: Findings and Lessons from Research in West-Africa." *JEID* 1(1):1–15.

Diagne, A. 2004. "Secondary Education in Senegal: Costs and Financing of a Sustainable Development." Proceedings of the Second Regional Convention of SEIA, Dakar, Senegal. The World Bank.

Docente Mas. 2006. "Sistema de Evaluación del Desempeño Profesional Docente." Chile: Government of Chile. Retrieved March 16, 2006 from http://www.docentemas.cl/index2.php

Duncan, W. 2000. "Basic Education in Indonesia: A Partnership in Crisis." In *Public-Private Partnerships in the Social Sector: Issues and Country Experiences in Asia and the Pacific*. Manila: Asian Development Bank Institute.

Education Standards Agency. 2003. *The National Inspection Programme Report*. Kampala: Government Press.

Figuerdo, V., and S. Anzalone. 2003. *Alternative Models for Secondary Education in Developing Countries; Rationale and Realities*. Washington, D.C.: IEQ Project.

Fiske, E. B. 1996. *Decentralisation of Education: Politics and Consensus*. Washington, D.C.: The World Bank.

Fretwell, D. H., and A. Wheeler. 2001a. *Hungary: Secondary Education and Training*. Washington, D.C.: The World Bank.

———. 2001b. *Russia: Secondary Education and Training*. Washington, D.C.: The World Bank.

Gershberg, A., and D. Winkler. 2003. "Education Decentralization in Africa: A Review of Recent Policy and Practice." Retrieved on November 19, 2004 from http://www1.worldbank.org/wbiep/decentralization/afrlib/winkler.pdf

Glatter, Ron, and others. 2005. "What's New? Identifying Innovation Arising from School Collaboration Initiatives." In *Educational Management Administration Leadership*. Sage Publications.

Govender, P., and P. Gruzd, eds. 2004. *Back to the Blackboard: Looking Beyond Universal Primary Education in Africa*. NEPAD Policy FOCUS Report I. Pretoria: SAIIA.

Government of South Africa. 2005. *White Paper on Education and Training Notice 196 of 1995*. Department of Education. Cape Town: Government Press.

———. 2006. Department of Education website. Retrieved March 16, 2006 from http://www.education.gov.za/

Greenaway, E. 1999. "Lower Secondary Education: An International Comparison." In *International Review of Curriculum and Assessment Frameworks*, Retrieved on July 15, 2005 from www.inca.org.uk/pdf/cav_final_report.pdf

Holsinger, D. B., and R. N. Cowell. 2000. *Positioning Secondary School Education in Developing Countries*. Paris: IIEP.

Hostens, G. 2001. *Educational Governance and Public Management Reforms*. Budapest: Institute for Educational Policy. Retrieved on July 15, 2006 from www.oki.hu

Independent Schools Inspectorate. 2006. Website. Retrieved March 16, 2006 from http://www.isinspect.org.uk/frreports.htm

Jansen, J., and N. Taylor. 2003. "Educational Change in South Africa 1994–2003: Case Studies in Large-Scale Education Reform." *Country Studies, Education Reform and Management Publication Series* 2(1).

Karlsen, G., and E. Sor-Trondelag. 1999. "Decentralized-Centralism Governance in Education: Evidence from Norway and British Columbia." *Canadian Journal of Educational Administration and Policy* 13.

Kellaghan, T., and V. Greaney. 1996. *Monitoring the Learning Outcomes of Education Systems*. Washington, D.C.: The World Bank.

———. 2003. *Monitoring Performance: Assessment and Examinations in Africa*. Paris: ADEA.

———. 2004. *Assessing Student Learning in Africa*. Washington, D.C.: The World Bank.

King, E., and B. Ozler. 1998. *What's Decentralization Got to Do with Learning? The Case of Nicaragua's School Autonomy Reform.* Washington, D.C.: The World Bank.

Kivuva, Leonora A. 2002. *Secondary Education Reform in Kenya: The Quest for Quality, Relevance, and Equity. Overview of Regional Secondary Education Reforms in the Nineties.* [Electronic Version]. Retrieved March 24, 2004 from www.ginie.org/cstudies/africa/cs-africa.htm.

Kruiter, A. 1995. *Good Governance for Africa: Whose Governance.* Maastricht: ECDPM. Retrieved March 16, 2006 from http://www.gdrc.org/u-gov/governance-understand.html

Lauglo, J. 2004. *Proceedings of Comparative International Education Society 2004: Vocationalized Secondary Education Revisited.* Washington, D.C.: The World Bank.

LeFloch, K. C., J. Taylor, and K. Thomsen. 2005. *The Implications of NCLB Accountability for Comprehensive School Reform.* Washington, D.C.: American Institutes for Research.

Lewin, K. M. 2000. *Linking Science Education to Labour Markets: Issues and Strategies.* Washington, D.C.: The World Bank.

———. 2004. "Beyond Primary Education for All: Planning and Financing Secondary Education in Africa (SEIA)." Paper presented at donor conference, The World Bank, Washington, D.C.

Liang, X. 2001. *China: Challenges of Secondary Education.* Washington, D.C.: The World Bank.

Linden, T. 2001. *Double-Shift Secondary Schools: Possibilities and Issues.* Washington, D.C.: The World Bank

McGinn, N. F. 2002. *International and National Trends in Local Governance of Education.* Paris: UNESCO.

Mediratta, K., and N. Fruchter. 2003. "From Governance to Accountability: Building Relationships that Make Schools Work." New York: NYU Institute for Education and Social Policy for the Drum Major Institute for Public Policy. Retrieved January 19, 2004 from www.drummajorinstitute.org/plugin/template/dmi

NIACE website. http://www.basic-skills-observatory.co.uk/uploads/doc_uploads/699.pdf.

Ndoye, Mamadou. 2004. "Secondary Education: The Missing Link." *ADEA Newsletter* 16(3):1–2.

North Central Regional Educational Laboratory. 2005. "Create a Clear and Focused Accountability System." Retrieved on July 1, 2005 from www.ncrel.org/sdrs/areas/issues

Nsubuga, Y. 2003. "Equitable Access and Management of Secondary Education in Uganda." Proceedings of First Regional SSA Conference for SEIA. Kampala.

Nyere, Julius. 1998. "Good Governance for Africa." Third World Network, Malaysia. Retrieved on November 19, 2004 from http://www.hartford-hwp.com/archives/30/083.html

OECD. 1994. *Vocational Education and Training for the 21st century: Opening Pathways and Strengthening Professionalism.* Proceedings of the Conference, The Changing Role of Vocational and Technical Education. Paris.

OECD. 2004. *OECD Information Technology Outlook 2004.* Paris.

———. 2004b. *OECD Survey of Upper Secondary School.* Paris.

———. 2005. *OECD Education at a Glance.* Paris.

Olowu, D., and S. Sako, eds. 2002. *Better Governance and Public Policy.* Kumarian Press.

Onsomu, E. N., M. J. Njoroge, D. Oulai, J. Sankale, and J. Mujidi. 2004. *Community Schools in Kenya: Case Study on Community Participation in Funding and Managing Schools.* Paris: UNESCO/IIEP.

Psacharopoulos, George, and M. Woodhall. 1985. *Education for Development: An Analysis of Investment Choices.* Washington, D.C.: The World Bank.

Quist, Hubert O. 2003a. "A Critical Appraisal of the Post-Colonial Context." *Africa Development,* 28(3&4):186–210.

Quist, Hubert O. 2003b. "Transferred and Adapted Models of Secondary Education in Ghana: What Implications for National Development?" *International Review of Education,* 49(5):411–31.

Republic of Kenya Ministry of Education. 2006. Website. Retrieved March 16, 2006 from http://www.education.go.ke/organandmanagement.htm

Republic of Senegal Ministry of Education. 2003. *Programme de développement de l'éducation et de formation (Education pour tous).* Dakar: Government Press.

Republic of Zambia. 2002. *Zambia Poverty Reduction Strategy Paper 2002–2004.* Ministry of Finance and National Planning. Lusaka.

Republic of Zambia Ministry of Education. 1996. *Educating Our Future: National Policy on Education.* Lusaka: Government Press.

Sagna, O. 2001. *Les technologies de l'information et de la communication et le développement social au Sénégal, Un état des lieux.* Dakar: UNRISD.

Seck, S. M., and C. Gueye. 2001. "Les nouvelles technologies de l'information et de la communication et le système éducatif." In *UNESCO World Education Report.* Paris: UNRISD.

SIMCE (Ministerio de Educacion Chile). 2006. Website. Government of Chile. Retrieved March 16, 2006 from http://www.simce.cl/paginas/presentacion.htm

Southern Africa Consortium for Monitoring Education Quality (SACMEQ). 2003. *Decentralization and Devolution of Control to Local Authorities: A proposal submitted to SADC Education Policy Support Initiative (EPSI).* Harare.

Stephens, Maria, and Jay Moskowitz, Jay. 2004. "Measuring Learning Outcomes in Developing Countries: A Primer." *EQUIP2 Issues Briefs.* Washington, D.C.: USAID.

UNDP. 1997. *Reconceptualising Governance.* Discussion Paper 2, Management Development and Governance Division, Bureau for Policy and Programme Support. New York.

UNESCO. 2006. *What is Secondary Education?* Secondary Education website. Retrieved March 16, 2006 from http://portal.unesco.org/education/en/ev.php-URL_ID=6343 &URL_DO=DO_TOPIC&URL_SECTION=201.html

UNESCO Institute of Statistics. 2001. Regional Report on Sub-Saharan Africa (Updated: 2005-03-18). Available at Statistics 2001- Regional Report on Sub-http://www.uis.unesco.org/ev.php?ID=4815_201&ID2=DO_TOPIC

UNESCO Institute of Statistics. 2005a. *Global Education Digest.* Montreal.

UNESCO Institute of Statistics. 2005b. Fact Sheet 04-05. Making the Transition to Secondary Education. Available at http://www.uis.unesco.org/ev.php?ID=6093_201&ID2=DO_TOPIC

UNESCO International Institute for Educational Planning. 2000. *IIEP Newsletter* 17(4):1.

Uganda Ministry of Education and Sports. 2002. *Options for Post-Primary Education and Training in Uganda.* Education Standards Agency, Kampala.

———. 2004. *Education Sector Annual Performance Report.* Kampala.

———. 2006. Website. Retrieved March 16, 2006 from http://www.education.go.ug/

Wang, Y., ed. 2000. *Public-Private Partnerships in the Social Sector: Issues and Country Experiences in Asia and the Pacific.* ADBI Policy Papers no. 1, Tokyo, Japan: Asian Development Bank.

Winkler, Donald R. 2004. "Strengthening Accountability in Public Education." *EQUIP2 Issues Briefs*. Washington, D.C.: USAID.

———. 2005. "Understanding Decentralization." *EQUIP2 Issues Briefs*. Washington, D.C.: USAID.

World Bank. 1994. *Governance: The World Bank's Experience*. Washington, D.C. Retrieved October 23, 2005 from www.gdrc.org/u-gov/governance-understand.html

———. 2005. *Expanding Opportunities and Building Competencies for Young People: A New Agenda for Secondary Education*. Directions in Development. Washington, D.C.: The World Bank.

———. 2006. *Education: Education and the World Bank Website*. Washington, D.C. Retrieved March 16, 2006 from http://web.worldbank.org/WBSITE/EXTERNAL/TOPICS/EXTEDUCATION/0,,menuPK:282391~pagePK:149018~piPK:149093~theSitePK:282386,00.html

———. 2007. *Recruiting, Retaining, and Retraining Secondary School Teachers and Principals in Sub-Saharan Africa*. World Bank Working Paper No. 99. Washington, D.C.

Eco-Audit
Environmental Benefits Statement

The World Bank is committed to preserving Endangered Forests and natural resources. We print World Bank Working Papers and Country Studies on 100 percent postconsumer recycled paper, processed chlorine free. The World Bank has formally agreed to follow the recommended standards for paper usage set by Green Press Initiative—a nonprofit program supporting publishers in using fiber that is not sourced from Endangered Forests. For more information, visit www.greenpressinitiative.org.

In 2007, the printing of these books on recycled paper saved the following:

Trees*	Solid Waste	Water	Net Greenhouse Gases	Total Energy
264	12,419	96,126	23,289	184 mil.
*40" in height and 6-8" in diameter	Pounds	Gallons	Pounds CO_2 Equivalent	BTUs

www.ingramcontent.com/pod-product-compliance
Lightning Source LLC
Chambersburg PA
CBHW081258170426
43198CB00017B/2833